THE MONKS OF NEW SKETE
DIVINE CANINE

The Monks' Way to a Happy, Obedient Dog

HYPERION
NEW YORK

Contents

THE MONKS' WAY

We live in a secluded, rural area, a traditional setting for many seeking the monastic life. As early morning sunlight peeks through a forest of birch, white pine and ash, it reveals the outlines of rustic monastery buildings trimmed in red, built by our own hands. Water falling into a fish pond quietly echoes through the stillness, and birds perch on the gilded domes sitting atop the steeply pitched roofs of Holy Transfiguration, one of two churches at our monastery. Gazing out our bedroom windows, we greet a brisk morning that reveals the bold colors of nature—a deep azure sky and, at this time of year, the myriad hues of the fall foliage. Could one ever tire of such beauty? The peacefulness is palpable, the quiet only enhanced by the sudden, brilliant sound of the monastery bells, calling us to matins, our morning prayer. We make our way to church as we do every morning, to offer our first thoughts and praises to God, who has orchestrated all this. Another day begins at New Skete.

But this is a special day, one of many special days that will both change and not change our normal routines. For today the first of a whole pack of visiting dogs will be arriving—their owners apprehensive as they prepare to turn over their beloved pets for an intensive four weeks of training.

There will undoubtedly be a fair amount of commotion, but all this is truly not unusual, not an intrusion at all. For more than 25 years, our community has supported itself, among other ways, by breeding and raising German shepherds, as well as training dogs of all breeds. And that peaceful solitude, on "normal" days, echoes not just with the sounds of bells and prayers, but also with the yapping of puppies and the barking of our monastery's own cadre of canines.

Over those many years, one lesson has become clear: Training dogs is about building a relationship that is based on respect and love and understanding. While New Skete has set itself on the margins of the world, our mission is still very much about making the world a better place—making all of our relationships, with humans and with animals, richer and stronger and more rewarding. We may not be *of* the world, but we are very much *about* the world. And the relationships we form with our dogs teach us a unique wisdom about living more fulfilling lives in that world. It pertains to what we call "life more abundant".

In raising and training our own German shepherds, we focus constantly on the bond between human and animal. It has been our experience that puppies who have close contact with humans right from the start have a much better chance of growing into well-adjusted dogs that are easy to train and wonderful to live with. But even with dogs who have not had that good beginning, in almost all cases the establishment, cultivation and ongoing development of a caring relationship still works wonders.

And the key to establishing a relationship is understanding. First, of course, it's important to understand the dog as a dog. Unfortunately, many dog owners, with the very best of intentions, view their dogs as little furry people with four legs. Let's be clear: Dogs are dogs, and their dignity lies precisely in that fact. Dogs don't have to become human to merit our esteem, and our relationships are much richer when we approach them as they are. They do have individual "personalities," and

"Dogs are the movers and shakers here."

different breeds have distinct characteristics, but fundamentally their motivations trace to the attributes of their species.

Like all dedicated dog professionals, then, we have worked hard to learn all we can about these marvelous creatures. We know their evolutionary trail, and we know their own history as a species. This knowledge informs the whole of our work, and we believe it is one reason why we have had success with our approach. But we are also mindful that any dog owner can understand a few simple truths about dogs that represent the keys to a successful relationship. In the most basic terms, two things stand out: Dogs are pack animals, and they thrive on a connection with people. It goes back to the prehistoric days when they first associated with humans, becoming their partners in the hunt and their companions around the fire.

What does their pack nature mean? It tells us that they look for their place in any group to which they belong. As you will see time and again in the stories in *Divine Canine*, many of the behavior problems owners struggle with result from the dog unintentionally being given a dominant place in the human family. We often see it as kindly to indulge our pets, but what we're really doing is giving them a mixed message. We're telling them they're literally the "top dog," and at the same time we're asking them to do as we say. No wonder they sometimes drive us crazy: We haven't properly communicated to them their rightful place.

So that's often how things can go wrong. But the other fundamental fact about dogs—their craving for a connection—is the secret to turning things right. When we show dogs in a genuine way that we love and respect them—not by coddling them but by understanding their true nature—they respond.

As you will learn in the stories to follow, anyone can make this work. Yes, there are some basic "tricks of the trade" that we'll explain. Vitally important is mastering the five essential obedience commands: sit, heel, stay, down and come; but equally essential is how these fit in with an entire mindset that takes into account the

whole dog: its needs and potential. You'll see the visiting dogs—and our own German shepherds—learn this approach as they go through their training. Then, as the tales unfold, you'll understand how a strong grasp of these skills, by both humans and dogs, can solve a host of behavior problems, from aggression and dominance to mouthing and just plain general misbehavior.

We are sometimes asked what sets us apart as trainers and breeders, and why we do it in the first place. The answer may sound simple, but it is the very essence of all we are about. We look for the divine in all God's creatures. We are here, we believe, to find and foster this awareness in all of us.

The sun is up, and we hear the sound of the first cars approaching. Come with us. It's time to meet the dogs.

The relationships we form with
our dogs teach us an earthy wisdom
about living in the world.

13

The Basics

Sit ○
Heel ●
Stay ●
Down ○
Come ○

TESSIE

Learning Who's in Charge

Tessie, a mini bull terrier, lives on Long Island with her owner, Maude. The problem? Role reversal: Tessie's the dominant member of this partnership. Our challenge is to teach Tessie her proper place, and to make clear to Maude that always being a pushover isn't doing her dog any favors.

One of Tessie's favorite things to do at home is go for walks on the beach with Maude. The windswept sands along the southern coast of Long Island in the small town of Point Lookout are a stone's throw from Maude's house, and walking there is a regular occurrence for Tessie—and a regular occasion for her to demonstrate her misbehavior.

We first encounter the problem side of Tessie—and, in a sense, of Maude—on a brisk, overcast day. The low waves crashing on the sand are the backdrop for some amusing antics that reveal a lot about this human-canine relationship. It all begins with a small piece of driftwood that becomes the centerpiece of a game of so-called "fetch." Actually, Tessie has the first part of fetch down pretty well. She dashes after the stick, sometimes even into the water, and snatches it up in a flash. She may even choose to come, if it catches her fancy. But the crucial last part—dropping the stick for Maude to throw again—clearly isn't in Tessie's plan. She much prefers a wrestling match with Maude, or sometimes a game of keep-away. Ultimately she sees the sense of letting Maude get the stick back, but only when Tessie is good and ready.

And then we notice something else. As Maude stops to talk, she has Tessie on the leash, and the stick is there on the sand, just out of Tessie's reach. She yaps at it, and strains on the leash, and Maude—who is involved in describing some of Tessie's less-than-pleasant behavior—gives in to the tugging just enough to let Tessie get to the stick. Then Maude yanks Tessie back, and Tessie strains again until she manages to pull Maude back close enough.

This happens again and again, and not just with the fetch toy. Maude tells Tessie it's time to go home, and Tessie heads in the other direction, either getting pulled back or, when Maude drops the leash to practice trying to get Tessie to come, running off just far enough to keep the dragging leash out of Maude's grasp. It's a constant battle of wills—and Maude is rarely winning.

"She can't be a good companion. It's like work bringing her out here," Maude says. "It's almost impossible to just relax with her, which is kind of sad, because she's a great dog, she's a lot of fun."

Tessie joined the family when she was eight weeks old—a reward for Maude's son for improving his grades—and struck everyone as lovable right from the start. The first sign of trouble, though, was that she was difficult to house-train. As she grew older, her energy level mushroomed, and "lovable" increasingly became replaced by "spunky." Maude never

took her for any formal obedience training, but she worked with her on her own, trying to teach her those well-known basics of sit, heel, and lie down. "She obeys when she wants to," Maude says, "which I guess isn't really obeying. I don't think she sees me as the boss. I think she sees Tessie as the boss. And she has to learn to reverse that." Such dominance extends to life in the house: Tessie makes the couch her place of choice, putting herself on Maude's level and intimidating her when Maude tries to move her off. Threatening growls are frequent enough and Tessie has snapped at Maude a number of times. On very real levels, Maude is afraid of Tessie.

Tessie loves to play games, and I love to play with her. But she's just not consistent when playtime's over, when it's time to behave."

—Maude

THE PROBLEM

Maude sees Tessie's problem as disobedience: not obeying commands. But in her descriptions of their relationship, Maude has also put her finger on the underlying behavioral problem: Tessie is the dominant member of this partnership.

Pack animals that they are, dogs need to know where they fit in the relationship. In the pack, they learn their place naturally through a continuous interaction with other pack members that involves play, challenges and roughhousing—finding out in the process who is dominant over whom, which fundamentally has to do with who gets to eat first. There is a clear pecking order. Tessie had done much the same thing in her human family. We'd seen it out there on the beach: challenging Maude over the stick, and running away when called, then teasingly coming back, only to dash off out of reach again. Without intending to, Maude had taught Tessie who was really in charge by continually letting Tessie win these contests, or at least not getting Tessie to do as she's told right away. Tessie would "get away with it" over and over, and Maude would simply give in.

There's no question that Tessie has a very general sense of the basic commands. But as Maude put it, "Tessie obeys only when she wants to."

Correcting the situation will involve not only training Tessie to obey commands unwaveringly, but also being sure Maude herself learns to lead effectively, to not give in to the challenges—to always get *her* way. Maude needs to change her behavior as much as Tessie does.

Tessie's Problems

- Pulling on the leash
- Not coming when called
- Jumping on people and knocking them over
- Not dropping a ball or stick
- Waking up "aggressive" from naps
- Obeying "only when she wants to"

AT THE MONASTERY

"Tessie loves car rides, and it will be a fun adventure for her when we drive up to the monastery," Maude says as she prepares for Tessie's four weeks of training at New Skete. "I'm going to be heartbroken when I leave her there, though. But I know it's worth it. And I'm looking forward to hearing what the monks have to tell me about managing an unmanageable dog. I'm willing to take any instruction they have to offer."

Maude's reaction in this regard is crucial, because it's essential to our approach that the owner be willing to take an active role in what is an ongoing process. All the instruction we give at the monastery will be for naught if the owner doesn't follow through. While their dogs are in training we recommend the owners read our books in preparation for the final demonstration, when they will be taught our approach in a very practical, hands-on way.

It's a widespread misconception that professional trainers can work their magic and return to you a dog that will respond to your every command just as she learned at obedience school—all you have to do is say, "Sit," or "Heel," or "Come." You have to give these brilliant creatures more credit than that. Not long after they get back to their old stomping grounds, they'll slip into their old bad habits if they find they can still get away with it.

We can't say it too many times: It's all about the relationship between the human and the canine. Both sides have to learn new ways.

The stakes are unquestionably high. According to Maude, Tessie has become increasingly hard to handle, has snapped at her, and has become so boisterous that she knocks visitors down. Maude can't even have her own mother over anymore because Tessie jumps all over her and could hurt her. Something has to give. Far too often, owners give up on dogs like Tessie, with heartbreak all around.

Part of the reason Tessie may be getting worse is that she herself is frustrated. Remember, Tessie sees herself as the dominant member of this "pack," so when Maude tries to get her to obey commands, or doesn't let Tessie do what she wants, it's Maude who is trying to subvert what Tessie sees as the natural order. After all, that's all that she's known. While Maude is complaining that Tessie is being disobedient, Tessie—in her own dogly way—is thinking the same thing about Maude.

So, our time with Tessie at New Skete will focus on shifting her out of this pattern, of "reminding" her, in the most literal sense of that word, that she is not the top dog in Maude's household. We need to restructure her mental image of the pack to which she belongs. But, of course, we will also have to transfer this to Maude, teaching her how to play the dominant role, making sure that she knows how to communicate properly with Tessie, how to enjoy her without indulging her, how to make clear to her that Maude's word is law. Tessie needs to learn who's in charge—but so does Maude. Without a disciplined understanding of basic obedience, both Maude and Tessie will continue to experience frustration.

What They're Thinking

TESSIE:
"I'm keeping this ball."

MAUDE:
"Tessie won't listen to me!"

THE MONKS:
"Tessie's in charge here. She's become dominant because Maude has let her win these contests too many times."

Before the Meeting

The dominance issue with Tessie continues even as Maude drives up the gravel road to the meeting area at the monastery. Tessie has her head out the half-open window—which Maude allows, but it's not something we recommend because dogs can get ear and eye problems with exposure to that much wind. As the car comes to a stop, Maude asks Tessie to sit; Tessie turns away from Maude, sticks her nose out the window again, turns back to look out the front window, and then finally decides to have a seat; Maude says, "Good girl!" but by this point, she's not praising obedience but actually reinforcing defiance.

Brother Christopher is waiting to greet them. As they've arranged, Maude gets out of the car first, leaving Tessie behind. It may seem only a gesture of politeness, but in our philosophy it's vitally important that Brother Christopher and Maude spend the first part of the interview talking about the positive aspects of Tessie before discussing problem behaviors, and that the introduction have its own peaceful pace.

Then Brother Christopher asks Maude to detail how Tessie's dominance expresses itself. It's important for him to understand all the misbehaviors involved, but in particular he's listening for several things: what's typical, what's extreme and most concerning, and how Maude understands and interprets this. The most troubling behavior is that Tessie can be aggressive, especially when she's been napping on the couch—or when she simply doesn't want to get off—and has snapped at Maude a few times. This is a potentially relationship-ending aspect of Tessie's dominance. But much of our work with Tessie will focus on fixing a behavior that represents her dominance more typically.

In simple terms, Tessie takes Maude for walks, not the other way around. She always leads, she determines the direction, and she sets the pace by constantly straining on the leash. As Brother Christopher puts it, "Sounds like Tessie's running the show."

Encouraging Maude

Tessie's training has yet to begin, but Maude's is already under way. Brother Christopher explains that he will talk with Maude by phone as Tessie's instruction progresses, and he will also provide her written information and videos of training sessions at the monastery to guide her when Tessie comes home. Maude knows that she needs to become the leader, but Brother Christopher senses an underlying concern and addresses it head-on.

"One of our biggest fears is that if we take charge, we're going to lose the dog that we love, that we're going to become this hard-edged owner who's making the dog miserable, and that the relationship is diminished." It's clear that this is exactly what's holding Maude back; she loves even the spunky aspects of Tessie and doesn't want to squelch them.

> "The bottom line is, for a successful relationship, you've got to be the leader."
> —Brother Christopher

Brother Christopher reassures her in the most confident terms. "Not at all, that's not what good obedience is about. Good obedience allows what you love about your dog to blossom. Once there's a foundation of obedience in place, you'll be able to address and correct problem behaviors when they arise without harming the bond of affection and fun-loving playfulness you clearly both enjoy."

"It sounds like a miracle," says Maude, but it's precisely how we expect things to go. A solid foundation and mastery of basic obedience allows good behaviors to blossom and problem behaviors to be diminished.

A kindly, gentle look tells the dog
that she is loved and accepted.

The Eyes Have It

With our own dogs, from the earliest days of pup-pyhood we stress the importance of contact between human and canine. Our puppies, after the first few weeks, are handled constantly and affectionately. But as important as this physical contact is, we put just as much effort into eye con-tact, which is key to establishing a relationship that will blossom as puppies grow into dogs.

Good eye contact serves several different purposes in the adult dog. A kindly, gentle look tells the dog that she is loved and accepted. But it is just as vital to communicate a stern reaction to bad behavior. A piercing, sustained stare into a dog's eyes tells her who's in charge; it establishes the proper hierarchy of domi-

nance between person and pet. We don't do this with anger, but with firmness. Such eye contact rivets the dog's attention and can help curtail unruly behavior. It also encourages respect and ensures that the dog is paying attention. A well-positioned training collar is the secret to establishing eye contact; lifting the dog's head up and keeping it firmly point-ed at your face virtually guarantees that the dog will look into your eyes.

TESSIE'S TRAINING

Now at last Brother Christopher and Tessie meet, and Brother Christopher instantly sees her charm, "but I see a bit of the devil in her as well." Tessie is exuberant, her tail wagging fiercely, and she seems overjoyed to greet this complete stranger. And then, almost right away, she lunges up at Brother Christopher. Maude pulls her back down, but Tessie gets her way and jumps again, and then again.

Because Brother Christopher is a complete stranger and there is no context of obedience between him and Tessie, he simply ignores the behavior. For leadership and corrections to be meaningful there has to be a context. In Tessie's case, Brother Christopher decides just to ignore the behavior for now. Although Tessie has an idea of some basic commands, we realize she will need to be treated as if she has learned nothing at all. In essence, she needs to be taken back to the beginning, to get a fresh start. So Brother Christopher lets Maude bid farewell, then he takes Tessie to her home for the next few weeks—the New Skete kennels.

Some people who have brought their dogs to us for training worry how their pets will adapt to a kennel environment, especially if they've never been exposed to one before. Dogs do have their own personalities, and some exhibit what in human terms we would call homesickness, even separation anxiety. But typically, the dog's social and adaptable nature makes this new experience something they adjust to quickly. Our kennels are large and open, with access to both indoor and outdoor areas. And there are lots of other dogs around, so there are plenty of new smells and new canine companions to become acquainted with.

We give Tessie a few days to get used to her new surroundings, in part so that she won't associate any of her training with the newness of her situation. She gets regular exercise, including walks, but nothing formal yet. Like most dogs, she adjusts well in those couple of days, and it's soon clear that she's ready for some obedience instruction.

At the very beginning, she is clearly testing her main handler, Brother Christopher, as well as others she works with. In her very first lessons, she borders on being belligerent. Brother Christopher uses firm correction—sharp pops on the leash—and doesn't allow any unruliness to continue. He simply keeps moving and reversing direction and doesn't allow Tessie to intimidate him with her belligerence. This isn't ballet at this stage, and Brother Christopher is careful not to get angry at her resistance. He keeps patiently working with her, trusting in the process and keeping in mind that the training will extend over the next month. No need to cram it all into one session. Tessie is quick to discover she's in a new situation, one she is not familiar with, and Brother Christopher will use this to give her a fresh start. Finally, she concedes: Tessie's ears move back submissively and she begins to pay closer attention to Brother Christopher's lead, warming a bit to his praise and encouragement.

WHAT IF tip

Maude is concerned about Tessie's tendency to wake up from a nap and be aggressive, even snappish. Knowing she's no longer the boss should keep Tessie from doing this, but what if she starts to act this way again after her training? First, it's not unusual for dogs to strike a defensive attitude if they're disturbed unexpectedly, so she should be given a gentle opportunity to awaken. If she does start to growl, the best approach is to give a firm verbal correction, and then to immediately give a basic command, such as "Come." To facilitate this, Maude should leave a leash on Tessie during naps, at least for a while. That way, the correction can be given quickly and surely and the bad behavior stopped in its tracks.

Tessie learning sit

Starting out from a brief period of walking at heel, Brother Christopher prepares to put Tessie into a sit by slowing down his pace (1). He brings his legs together as he stops and attracts Tessie's attention (2). By lifting up the leash, he gets Tessie to go into a sit (3). Later, she will sit automatically when he comes to a stop.

Success with Heel and Stay

Once she understands that, as Brother Christopher puts it, "there's a new marshal in town," Tessie begins to respond more consistently. She's fairly good at sitting, so her drills concentrate on the other basic commands: heel, stay, down and come. Brother Christopher works with her in a paved exercise yard just outside the kennels—a relatively small area with no distractions. She wears a training collar that Brother Christopher makes sure is snug around the upper part of her neck, just behind her ears. He tells her to sit, at the same time passing his hand in front of her face and lifting up gently on the leash, which automatically forces Tessie's butt down and turns her head up so that she makes eye contact (see "The Monks' Way," pages 32-33). He holds the pose for a few seconds, not giving Tessie any opportunity to move out of position.

It's restraint, but nothing that hurts her, and it's not a correction or a punishment. This sort of control is a vital first step in obedience training. Tessie is being good because she just physically can't do anything else at the moment.

Brother Christopher reinforces with verbal praise, then simultaneously gives the "Heel" command and starts walking, keeping Tessie right beside him by ensuring that there's a slight amount of slack on the leash. The slack allows Tessie the freedom to make a mistake by trying to advance out in front. But Brother Christopher is leading this walk, setting the pace and establishing which way they will go. To reinforce this, he changes direction unexpectedly, still keeping Tessie close, making her pay close attention. She quickly learns that she can go nowhere else except where Brother Christopher is heading—and she gets praise for being there beside him, even though she has no other choice!

"You're not going to instantly have a ready-made robot that will obey your every command. Training is a function of your relationship, and that's an ongoing process."

—Brother Christopher

When she occasionally tries to strain away, he gives a short, sharp "No" and a corrective pop on the leash—a quick gesture that brings her back in line without pulling or dragging her. It's a no-nonsense move that tells Tessie there's no game going on here, no contest to be won or lost, no tug-of-war between equals.

For the next fifteen minutes the drill goes on. They walk with Tessie at heel, then she is told to sit and made to do so with the leash and training collar. She occasionally—but not every time by any means—gets a food reward, and the verbal praise keeps coming; in the sit position she will also get a pleasurable rub on the chest every so often.

About halfway through, Brother Christopher gives Tessie the "Stay" command. It comes on her almost before she knows what is happening, and that's part of the secret. With her sitting, Brother Christopher raises his hand—from which he has just dispensed a treat—and holds it palm outward in front of her face; he says "Stay" and slightly releases the tension on the leash. Then he quickly walks around her twice, ready to correct her if necessary—but it isn't. Tessie is probably still thinking about the possibility of a treat, but she's also not exactly sure what's going on, and that's to the trainer's advantage. Already, this simply, he has established dominance.

The next time he tells her to stay, she does test the limits, and she gets the corrective pop on the leash.

All the essentials of obedience training are right here in this lesson: communicating authority, keeping the dog's attention focused, giving clear commands a minimum number of times, lavishing encouragement and praise, and perhaps most important of all, allowing only proper behavior through a combination of restraint and correction.

Tessie and Treats

"I used treat rewards with Tessie a little more at the beginning, and a little more than I normally would," Brother Christopher notes. "In the case of a dog who has been dominating her family, the transition to a training regimen can be a downer—it's clearly not as much fun to be the follower rather than the leader. So, to get the most out of our training sessions, in the beginning I encouraged her with more frequent food rewards to get her going. She already knew she wasn't going to get away with anything with me; the treats simply reinforced that this new order of things had a distinct up side. Then I gradually weaned her off them and concentrated exclusively on praise."

Tessie's Progress

Over the next couple of weeks the lessons continue at least twice a day, for no more than fifteen minutes at a time. Short, peppy lessons done more frequently are much more effective in training than one long session. She also gets to play and to have unstructured time with us in the afternoon. The initial successes with heel and stay become the foundation for teaching her the "Come" and "Down" commands. We also work in combinations of these commands, and she becomes proficient at sit-stay and down-stay.

The progression involves maintaining leadership while keeping the leash slightly slack. Tessie learns to stay and then come while attached to a long leash, but soon the leash can be dropped altogether. Tessie is motivated to do the right thing. She knows what her place is with us, and she has learned that it comes with positives.

Repetition, reinforcement and correction have made things work with Tessie, but behind it all is the reestablishment of the proper human-canine

relationship. Tessie is a smart dog—with few exceptions they all are—and she learns quickly. She knows that her trainers at New Skete are in charge, that she's not the dominant one, and that has made all the difference.

Remember These Things

- [ ] Be effusive with verbal praise.
- [ ] Reward with treats only occasionally.
- [ ] Use gentle restraint to prevent bad behavior.
- [ ] Correct bad behavior right away and firmly.

TESSIE TRANSFORMED

Tessie's training at the monastery is over, and Maude has come to pick her up. Before they greet each other again, though, Maude needs to go through verbal instruction with Brother Christopher and then to see for herself the progress that Tessie has made. It's in part to help Maude learn how to give proper commands to Tessie, but it's also to reinforce with Maude that things are different now, and that she needs to change as well.

"One of the challenges I see ahead is Maude's soft heart," says Brother Christopher. "The jury is still out as to whether Maude will really be able to trust the prescription for improved behavior."

Maude is understandably anxious and excited to see Tessie again, but we want to be sure Maude sees a focused Tessie going through her paces first. So Maude watches from inside as Brother Christopher leads Tessie through her newly mastered commands.

Tessie does wonderfully, and Maude is suitably impressed. "I can't get over how obedient she is, and how calm," she comments. At least at the outset, she too is highly motivated to keep the progress going.

That unexpressed fear that the old Tessie will have been transformed into a well-behaved but different and less fun-loving creature is set aside as soon as they see each other. The greeting is exuberant, and Tessie is wagging her tail so hard that her whole body wriggles back and forth. The joy has demonstrably not been trained out of this little bundle of energy.

But will Maude be able to follow through? She realizes that Brother Christopher has established himself as benevolently dominant over Tessie. But will Maude be able to do the same?

Maude has the tools at her disposal. She has materials from us, including video of Tessie's training, that will enable her to use the proper obedience command techniques. And Brother Christopher has frequently discussed with her the importance of being firm and in charge. "No more napping on the couch for Tessie," he has told her. "It puts her on your level, and she needs, from now on, to be subservient to you. If you need to build your confidence indoors, use a short leash initially with Tessie in the house. It doesn't mean you can't have fun with her. In fact, if you stick to the training and practice every day, you'll have much more fun with her. She'll be the companion you wanted her to be—if you can stick to being top dog."

"Tessie really is transformed. She listens to me now, and she respects me."

—Maude

Maude has her doubts, but before they head home, Brother Christopher watches as Maude directs Tessie through some of the basic commands. Tessie obeys flawlessly, and Brother Christopher is there as always with verbal praise and encouragement. It's as much for Maude as for Tessie. "Maude needs her own self-confidence reinforced," he notes.

Back at home, Maude does follow through, and works with Tessie every day. She no longer allows Tessie to sleep on the bed or nap on the couch, and both members of this loving relationship are comfortable with the arrangement. The worrisome aggressiveness has disappeared.

"But I do see that it's work," Maude says. "If I become less consistent, or if I forget to do our little training sessions, she could revert. It's work, but it's well worth it."

The important thing here is that Maude now has the focus on her own behavior as much as on Tessie's. And once again she sees the best that Tessie can be.

"She's fun, lovable, gentle, feisty but obedient! I'm looking forward to a good relationship."

Q&A:
Your New Dog

We saw some adorable purebred puppies for sale from someone's home. But we've also been thinking about rescuing a shelter dog. How do we decide where to get a new dog?

Your desire for a dog is, we'd humbly offer, a sign of how good-hearted you are. But let your head, not your heart, guide you in the actual decision-making process. Plan your adoption carefully, studying characteristics of different breeds to determine what type of dog might be right for your circumstances. And don't fall prey to making a quick, emotional purchase, whether from a pet store, a backyard breeder, or even the animal shelter—it's almost never a wise move.

Of the main sources, we'd have to say it's best to avoid pet stores, which tend to get dogs from puppy mills, outfits that mass-produce puppies with minimal attention to important details of breeding and socialization. The same goes for backyard breeders, who often know little about proper breeding and puppy-handling. As for animal shelters, your urge to rescue is certainly noble, and many wonderful dogs come from shelters. But you should be aware that you may not get any background information, so you have little to guide you on a dog's temperament or health history (it might, for example, be incubating a virus if it wasn't properly vaccinated). If you do adopt from a shelter, consider asking for help from an independent expert, or wait until you're experienced and can handle what might be a more difficult dog.

It should be no surprise that we recommend that you turn to an experienced breeder with a solid reputation, who will know the given breed and its characteristics intimately, will be current on all vaccinations and have taken time on socialization. A good professional breeder will also be a valuable resource in the future for questions that might arise.

What do I need to know about bringing a new dog into my home if I already have another dog—how should I introduce them to each other?

First and foremost, you need to be realistic about your present dog's character. Do you know for certain that he's already dog-friendly? If you're not sure, work with a professional trainer, who can help your dog learn to interact well with other dogs.

As for the introduction itself, stage it at a neutral location, away from your present dog's "home." You'll need one other person to help. Have both dogs on leashes and let them sniff each other first. Then take them both on a walk and allow them to interact informally. Don't try too hard to make them "like" each other. Project a certain matter-of-fact confidence and leadership and let them adjust to each other gradually.

Once they are used to each other's presence, you can take them back to your home together. Then keep the attention you show each dog balanced. Have their crates next

to each other. Feed them in their crates (at least initially) and take each dog out for separate sessions with you. It's important to establish and maintain a bond with each dog or they will tend to bond with each other and ignore you.

If the new dog is a puppy, don't dote on it. Keep the pup from pestering your first dog as much as you can.

I'm away at work nine hours a day. Can I even have a dog?

You have to be utterly honest with yourself and willing to sacrifice. Dogs are social creatures; they require "quality" time, even if you aren't able to spend as much as some owners. You must be willing to walk and train your dog before and after work, for 15 to 30 minutes each time. Are you up for

that? Are you willing to spend special time on weekends that includes more formal training? Are you willing to hire a dog walker, pet sitter, or doggie day care to address your dog's needs while you're away? Only if you can sincerely pledge to do these things should you consider getting a dog.

The Basics
Sit ●
Heel ○
Stay ●
Down ○
Come ●

HUGO

A Bull-Headed Bulldog

Like most bulldogs, Hugo is actually a sweetie pie—loyal and loving and playful. But there's one way in which he lives up— or down—to his breed's name. Hugo's owners have struggled mightily with basic obedience commands, and can't seem to stop him from jumping up on people. He has another "difficulty" up his sleeve as well. To put it diplomatically, Hugo can sometimes be just a little too loving.

There are two types of people in this world: those who know about bulldogs, and those who don't. If you're already familiar with these marvelous creatures, we need say no more. If you're not, you should know that bulldogs are among the most affectionate and loyal of breeds. Their gruff exterior belies their truly sweet nature.

And so it is with Hugo, who lives with his owners, Leroy and Katina, in Maryland. They've had him for three years now and continue to enjoy all those admirable qualities—the devotion, the affection, the playfulness. But they have also witnessed quite a transformation in that time. When they first got him, at eight weeks old, he seemed like the perfect dog. "What a sweet, gentle, calm animal he was," Katina recalls of those first few blissful days. "We were lulled into thinking that it'd be like this forever." It wasn't long, though, until another side of Hugo emerged.

While Hugo was still small, the problem wasn't that much of a concern.

His rambunctiousness was reasonably enough tabbed as mere puppy exuberance, something he would undoubtedly outgrow. In fact, seeing this little bundle with the Winston Churchill face lavish affection on friends and family alike, bouncing from one person to another and jumping all over the place, just seemed to spread joy through the house.

Bulldogs never get that big height-wise, but they are as solid as rocks—or as linebackers, which is the more appropriate metaphor in Hugo's case. At his "playing weight" of 65 pounds, Hugo now packs a wallop, and visitors stand little chance of keeping their feet when Hugo comes rushing to greet them. Because he's low to the ground, people often hunker down to say hello, and Hugo's front-paws-first greeting almost always floors them.

Not that it's really any better to stand tall against him. You see, Hugo has another version of the over-the-top greeting, and it's a constant source of embarrassment for his owners and annoyance for their friends. Hugo's jump up against the leg quickly turns into a grab, as he clings on with his front paws, and . . . well, Katina and Leroy usually stop things at that point by dragging Hugo away by the leash. But the damage is already done. Nobody much appreciates a dog that seems to have his basic instincts so much to the fore.

Compounding the problem is that Hugo knows his own mind and cares not at all for anyone else's opinion. In a word, Hugo is stubborn. It is indeed an aspect of the breed—one that can be dealt with, but Katina and Leroy have clearly had no success overcoming it. So when Hugo goes into his greeting routine, his owners have few options beyond leaving the scene. "Training" has increasingly become equivalent to avoidance, with the result that Hugo is becoming increasingly marginalized from their daily lives.

"It's gotten to the point that we can't do any of the fun things with Hugo anymore," says Katina, "like go to the dog park. You get the sense that other people are looking at you and saying, 'I wish they would just take their dog and go home.'"

THE PROBLEM

Much like Tessie (see pages 22-43), Hugo's main, underlying problem is dominance. He sees himself as the leader of his family's pack. When Leroy takes him for a walk, for example, he pulls continuously on the leash, and is always out in front. This is his way of saying he's in charge, that he's the ranking member of the group. When Leroy tells him to sit, Hugo just stands there looking up at Leroy, not with defiance as much as with disdain and lack of interest.

Hugo's dominance has the added burden of breed stubbornness to it. Where Tessie would eventually decide, in her own good time, that she was ready to sit, with Hugo it is different: Since Katina and Leroy's commands are excessively verbal and repetitive and carry no physical follow-through (in the sense of making Hugo comply), Hugo is left free to make his own decisions. More often than not he simply ignores the command. Say "Sit" and he blows you off: When commanded to do so, it's the very last thing he'd ever contemplate. He'll stand till the cows come home.

Hugo's other major problem, which we in the trade call mounting behavior, also has ancestral roots and is not uncommon in unneutered males. Hugo will be neutered after his training time at New Skete, but that alone will not solve the problem. Unless corrective action is taken, his mounting behavior would probably reemerge even though it no longer has a hormonal, biological drive behind it. The action itself of grabbing on to a person's leg has become habitual, Hugo's form of greeting; it's a patterned behavior whose initial hormonal trigger has now simply become Hugo's "m.o." The challenge of his training will be to break that pattern by teaching him a new set of expectations when he greets people.

Hugo's Problems

- Jumping up and tackling visitors
- Grabbing legs
- Not obeying the basic commands
- Always pulling on a walk

AT THE MONASTERY

The day for Hugo's training to begin has arrived, and Katina and Leroy are understandably anxious, despite the reassurances we've given them in preparatory interviews. "When we went on our honeymoon," Katina remembers, "my parents said he would just sit in the house and stare at the door. I felt so guilty! And now I'm having the same kind of separation anxiety."

This is a common reaction among good and caring dog owners, but it's important not to project our own human emotions onto dogs, reading into them all manner of things that aren't really there. In his first few days in the monastery's kennel, Hugo is not going to be sitting there thinking, "Okay, where's my cell phone so I can call my lawyer—he needs to get me out of here!"

> ## "Hugo's stubbornness is not just irritating. It's potentially dangerous."
>
> —Brother Christopher

Not at all. Dogs just aren't that way. One of the things that's absolutely beautiful about dogs is that they are very much creatures of the present. Granted, at first Hugo will understand that the kennel is not home and experience a mild disorientation. However, that will quickly pass as he adapts to the new present he will be living in. At most the adjustment will be a couple of days.

Still, after a ten-hour drive from their home in Maryland, Katina and Leroy can't entirely quell their doubts—or stop turning Hugo into a human being. "He's going to be upset with us and miss us, he's going to be angry with us," says Leroy as they drive up to the monastery. "Of course he's going to miss us," says Katina. "I just hope that he doesn't hate the training. He's not really the school type."

They constantly try to reassure Hugo as they arrive. We are well aware, however, that it's themselves who really need the reassuring.

Getting to know you

The first couple of days are always a kind of gentle transition into the training regimen. And that all begins with the first meeting. Brother Christopher greets Hugo warmly on the grassy lawn and immediately gets down to his level. This is, in fact, already the beginning of training, for he is preventing Hugo from jumping up and going into his normal dominance routine with strangers. With a gentle hand, Brother Christopher keeps Hugo down.

From the very first moment with Hugo, we work to establish a relationship, and at the same time we remind the owners that this is a training bond, one that will not in any way compromise or replace their own loving relationship with their dog. Hugo is simply learning from the start that Brother Christopher is kind but firm—and clearly in charge.

Stubbornness wouldn't be stubbornness, though, if it wasn't hard to overcome, and Hugo will be trying to put us through our paces, quite literally, as we work to break his negative patterns. After Brother Christopher's initial success at keeping him down, Hugo is up to his typical tricks even before his owners have made their goodbyes, barreling into the nearest set of legs and doing his best to get a grip—which we refuse to let him do. But the testing will go on well into his training.

"Hugo's stubbornness is not just irritating," Brother Christopher notes. "It's also potentially dangerous." The combination of a dog who knocks people over and also won't listen could lead to very real physical harm—to an old person or a child, for instance—even though there clearly isn't an aggressive bone in Hugo's solid little body. He wouldn't mean it, but his, well, dogged refusal to respond to commands could actually hurt someone.

During the acquaintance phase of our relationship with Hugo, we find that he has another aspect to his personality that could complicate the training process. "It's the couch potato factor," says Brother Christopher. Training always goes better when the dog is motivated,

What They're Thinking

HUGO:
"Howdy! I like you!"

KATINA AND LEROY:
"This is so embarrassing!"

THE MONKS:
"Hugo has turned a natural urge into a patterned greeting. That pattern has to be broken."

THE MONKS' WAY

The Lowdown on Jumping Up

Jumping up is one of the most problematic behaviors dog owners face. The fault often traces to the way a dog was handled in its first few months of life. At the monastery with our own German shepherds, we take steps from the earliest days of puppyhood to habituate our dogs to a life lived close to the ground. We start playing with the puppies down on the ground, and although we do indulge in the occasional embracing cuddle up in our arms, we try to keep this to a minimum. We introduce collars and leashes while stretched out on the floor, and we never do anything to encourage the puppies to reach up. As they get older and more formal training commences, we do teach them to look up at us from a sitting position,

but any move to rear up on hind legs is discouraged. Needless to stay, we never allow puppies or dogs on furniture.

All this makes jumping up a nonissue, and also confirms the dog's place in the relationship. Jumping up can be trained away, as Hugo will prove, but it can also be prevented in the first place.

The absolutely beautiful thing about dogs is
that they are very much creatures of the present.

whether by verbal praise, occasional treats, or affectionate handling. It may be part of his adjustment to a new environment, but initially there just isn't very much enthusiasm in Hugo, for anything at all. No, he's not looking for his cellphone to call his lawyer, but when we go to the kennels to take him out for an initial training session, he'd clearly rather stay where he is. "Oh, please," we imagine him saying as he shifts his head from side to side, "you've got to be kidding."

All joking aside, it's important not to take our playful humanizing of Hugo's reaction too seriously. But there's no denying that we will need to work on stirring his interest to get the training to stick.

HUGO'S TRAINING

Our plan with Hugo is to combine an animated, peppy approach with limited food reinforcement to help him into the rhythm of twice-daily training sessions that will be kept purposefully brief; it's a lot easier to keep a dog's focus and interest for ten minutes than a half hour. Dogs are definitely creatures of habit—which can be both to their detriment and to their benefit. Hugo's bad habits are why he's here, but his natural tendency to respond in patterned ways may help enable him to become an exceptionally well-behaved canine, one who *never* jumps up and *never* grabs—indeed stubbornly and reliably so. If we can successfully correct his old ways and repeat, repeat, repeat new ones, we could help that wonderful other side of stubbornness—better known as dependability—come out in Hugo.

Part of the challenge with Hugo is that he needs intensive work in just about every one of the basic commands; he is, by and large, an untrained pooch and he's already close to two and a half years old. Ironically for a dog who jumps up, the one command we won't be focusing on at first is "Down." That will come further on in the training. For a dog of his body type—stocky and short-necked—a full lie-down position can make it slightly harder for him to maintain eye contact with the handler, and eye contact is one of the issues we need to address with him in a manner that reinforces human leadership.

But we will try to get into the other four basic exercises quickly: heel, sit, stay, and come. And heel is the first we work on.

Some people think heel is one of the more advanced commands because it seems to require such precise control of the animal. With Hugo, that's exactly the point. Heel is indeed a control exercise, and it's by far the best way to manifest leadership to a dog who's been taking that role for himself. Also, it is easier to begin working with a dog while the dog is moving, rather than to attempt a static exercise such as sit or stay. However, when a dog hasn't had any real foundation in leash work, rather than trying to introduce a formal heel, we begin the process with "Let's go," a more relaxed command that gently eases the dog into familiarity with the leash and cooperation in walking with the owner.

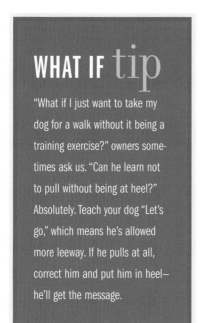

WHAT IF tip

"What if I just want to take my dog for a walk without it being a training exercise?" owners sometimes ask us. "Can he learn not to pull without being at heel?" Absolutely. Teach your dog "Let's go," which means he's allowed more leeway. If he pulls at all, correct him and put him in heel—he'll get the message.

Starting with Heel

Thus, for the first two days, Brother Christopher simply takes Hugo out to get him used to the leash and collar, walking him back and forth informally using the "Let's go" command, the goal of which is to keep the dog walking without pulling, whether he is smelling the ground or not. Brother Christopher keeps things relaxed and informal and uses these occasions to help Hugo get familiar with him and his way of walking with the leash.

Once these sessions are completed, Brother Christopher brings a somewhat familiarized Hugo out to the exercise yard and guides him into an initial sit by applying light pressure on his rear end. After making sure Hugo's collar (a good dog collar [see page 141] that doesn't rub his sensitive skin) is positioned properly, he gives a chipper "Heel!" command and an encouraging slap on his thigh and keeps Hugo close to the side of his leg with the leash slightly slack—so that he'll understand what heel means. After several paces Hugo begins to move out in front and Brother Christopher allows the leash to extend to its full length, then immediately gives a quick pop to the leash while simultaneously saying "No!" shortly and sharply, or an equally unpleasant, bitten-off "Eh!" correction.

But most important of all, Brother Christopher immediately turns 180 degrees in the opposite direction, keeping a fair amount of slack on the leash after the pop. This is the absolutely crucial detail for a dog like Hugo. The point is for him to see the human out in front, being the leader. That's where Hugo has always been, but now he must learn the new pattern. Brother Christopher repeats the encouraging, upbeat "Heel!" and shortens his grip on the leash as Hugo comes up beside him.

Again and again they go through this routine: close heel, slight straying, verbal "No!" simultaneous with the leash correction and then an immediate turn in the opposite direction, followed by immediate and sincere praise. If you're doing this with your own dog, you'll quickly see that it's best to be in an area that you reserve for training rather than out on a "linear" walk; you want your dog to stay focused, and you definitely want to be able to make frequent changes of direction so that the dog has to learn to follow your lead.

Casual Time

Because of Hugo's tendency to be unenthusiastic, Brother Christopher keeps the sessions short and upbeat. It's easier to keep the dog's focus and attention this way. He'll also vary the intensity, occasionally beginning a session with a bright "Let's go!" then slapping his thigh three or four times with an encouraging jiggle on the leash. This is a sign to

Hugo that things are temporarily going to be more relaxed and casual, that he'll have an opportunity to sniff around a bit. So Brother Christopher gives him more slack and allows Hugo to get his nose to the ground and go, ever so slightly, his own way. But as soon as there is the least dragging on the leash from Hugo's end, he gets an immediate correction and is then given the more formal heel command.

This is an important distinction, and one that reassures many owners. No, your dog doesn't always have to be in Marine Corps lockstep when you go on a walk. Dogs do need to get a chance to investigate their surroundings, and few people really want a little robot at their side all the time. The trick is, you have to be able to get your dog into heel when you need to, and to teach him never to pull, never to drag you. Varying the "Heel" and "Let's go" commands during training sessions will help your dog understand the difference.

Hugo's Progress: Sit, Stay, Come

Despite all early signs to the contrary, Hugo does make steady progress, and he's continually showing more interest in training—and in being a good boy. Brother Christopher is able to move to "Sit" and "Stay," and Hugo picks up on the commands surprisingly quickly.

All these commands are of practical value on their own, but they also target Hugo's problems of dominance and jumping-grabbing. Heel has worked to teach Hugo that he's not the one in the lead. Sit and stay, when perfected, will make it much harder for him to jump up on people—they are control positions that make it harder for dogs like Hugo to jump up once they have been commanded to stay in the sit-stay position.

Brother Christopher moves fairly quickly into teaching "Come." He uses a six-foot leash, and after putting Hugo in a sit-stay, backs away from him with his hand held up, palm facing Hugo, to the end of the leash. Before Hugo breaks the "Stay," which, happily, he is holding for longer and longer, Brother Christopher tells him to come and gives a

Hugo masters sit-stay-come

After putting Hugo in a sit, Brother Christopher keeps Hugo in the stay position by holding the leash high (1). He begins to move away, keeping Hugo's attention with a hand gesture (2). The leash dropped, Hugo stays (3) until getting the command to come (4). The lesson ends with praise (5).

slight, encouraging tug to the leash. When Hugo gets to him, Brother Christopher puts him immediately into a sit and praises him effusively, patting him upwards from the chest and sometimes adding a treat. Again and again they do this, with only the occasional correction when he tries to bound beyond Brother Christopher or jump up on him. Hugo gets it quickly. Very soon the leash can be left lying on the ground and Hugo comes to Brother Christopher with only the verbal encouragement. And very soon after that he will come even as Brother Christopher is backing away from him, to a greater and greater distance. While Brother Christopher uses a 50-foot rope clipped to the leash as a precaution, it's still quite impressive.

But it's not perfect yet. There's still a stubborn edge to some of Hugo's responses. Sometimes when he comes to a trainer and sits, he turns his head away and refuses to make eye contact. "I have to laugh,"

says Brother Christopher. "There's something about him that reminds me of the crusty old vaudevillian Jimmy Durante singing, 'I gotta be me!'"

That's part of Hugo's charm, and so long as it doesn't lead him to disobey when he gets a firm command, it's not a problem.

Round-Robin Recall

One of the ways we reinforce the "Come" command is with an exercise called Round-Robin Recall. It takes at least two people and a long training leash—about 50 feet—that has a weight at the end opposite the collar clasp. (You can tie a length of rope to a regular leash and loop a small weight at the other end.) Hugo seems to love this drill, and it helps cement his progress. One trainer puts Hugo into a sit-stay, then tosses the weighted end of the rope to the other trainer, who then calls

Hugo. If he doesn't respond right away, or if he doesn't head directly to the other trainer, he gets a corrective pop on the leash to get him in line and refocus his attention. When he gets to the second trainer, he's brought into a sit-stay; the leash goes flying in the opposite direction, and he gets another "Come!" command. About five minutes of this back and forth is the limit, but it proves to be an excellent way to get Hugo into the habit of coming to both owners when called.

Passing "the Test"

We've been careful through the first two weeks of Hugo's training to give him virtually no opportunity to jump up on people or grab a leg. Remember, his most annoying misbehavior was this patterned form of greeting strangers. We needed to change his whole mindset on this, so we've kept his handlers to a minimum—no strangers allowed—all in service of breaking the pattern. Now it's time to put his progress to the test, and also to establish a new pattern for him to follow.

We design a kind of real-world scenario: Brother Christopher walks along with Hugo, and someone Hugo is unfamiliar with comes walking in the opposite direction. The first few times they just walk past each other, with a greeting but no further interaction. If Hugo shows the slightest interest in the stranger, he gets a quick leash correction to the side and on they go. After a few times like this, Brother Christopher

> ### Remember These Things
> - Use a short, sharp "No!" or "Eh!" with leash pop.
> - To be in the lead, turn in the opposite direction suddenly.
> - Do training in an area with minimal distractions.
> - Never use dog's name with "No!"

greets the "stranger" more warmly, and they stop beside each other for a moment. Hugo is given just enough leeway to be able to do what he used to.

And the first time or two, Hugo does jump up, his stubby tail wagging profusely. Brother Christopher corrects him the moment it occurs with a "No! Off!" and puts him into a sit-stay. He gets a clipped "good boy" without any petting, and then they walk on after only a few seconds. It's key here that Hugo be corrected, that he learn his old behavior is just plain not acceptable.

They do this over and over and over again, and Hugo gets better and better. Eventually the two people are able to stand and talk for several minutes while Hugo sits there patiently. The best sign of all is that he is clearly happy to see this new person—his tail is doing the best it can to wag what little it has—but he makes no move to jump up. He has, it seems, developed a new greeting habit.

HUGO TRANSFORMED

Katina comes to pick Hugo up after four weeks, and she watches from inside while Brother Christopher shows off what Hugo has learned. She's mightily impressed, and excited beyond her own expectations to see her little troublemaker again.

As she watches from a window, Hugo begins to turn his head in her direction. Has he sensed her presence? There's little doubt that he has, even though he can't see her. Perhaps he has caught her scent. No matter. We witness this frequently, and it's an encouraging sign that the family bond is still almost mystically strong—the power of things

"The word that best describes our approach
to training is holistic. It's not just exercises—
it's about a whole life with your dog."

—Brother Christopher

unseen. But the real question of the moment is: Will Hugo go back to form when he sees Mommy again?

After the demonstration, we tell Katina to go outside, and here comes Hugo, barreling in. Will he tackle her? Following our instruction, she has gotten in a stable position on the ground, and Hugo comes in low himself, nuzzling up to her, his back end all one big wag. He rolls for a tummy rub, and she nuzzles into him as well—the love they feel for each other as strong and warm and ebullient as ever.

But it doesn't degenerate. After a brief settling down period, Katina stands, and Hugo sits. Directed by Brother Christopher, she takes Hugo's leash and tells him to heel, and he does, looking up at her as he gaits. He sits on command—several times in succession—and then stays . . . and comes when called, even sitting smartly at its finish. He's got it all.

Katina and Hugo head home, ready for more tests. He greets Leroy as warmly as he did Katina, but he doesn't go too far—no jumping. They call in a friend, and almost before they can give the command, Hugo parks his butt and stays in place, stubby tail aflutter. He is happy and good and—yes, dependably—sticking to the new pattern.

Both Katina and Leroy realize they have to keep working with Hugo, and they plan on each taking a daily follow-up session of fifteen minutes for the next three weeks. "We have to do it," says Leroy, "or it's going to go back to how it used to be." That might be true, and it might not. We do have a lot of confidence that Hugo's bull-headedness has been turned to the good, that he will reliably stick to his new ways. But we also believe that lifelong learning is a guarantee against any backsliding. What's more, Hugo clearly is capable of stretching his behavioral horizons, and both he and his family have the potential of enriching their relationship for long days to come.

"A dog who is educated to life," says Brother Christopher, "who is continually learning new things—that's a happy, well-adjusted dog, becoming who he's supposed to be."

Q&A:
What's Up, Pup?

I've never house-trained a puppy before. What do I need to know? And what's this about "crating"?

Don't be too intimidated about house-training. A dog's natural instincts to keep its den area clean, coupled with your own understanding and consistency, will help make the process predictable and straightforward.

First, we recommend that you use a crate when house-training. Remember that dogs are den animals and actually enjoy spots that are safe and secure. A crate also prevents a pup from getting into mischief when she can't be watched—and, of course, because your puppy wants to keep her "den" clean, the crate helps you control when she relieves herself.

Keep the crate near the door where your puppy will go outside, and feed her in the crate. Make a schedule for feeding and taking her outside, and be vigilant about sticking to it—consistency is all in house-training. Your pup will want to relieve herself when she wakes in the morning or after a nap, shortly after she eats, and after exercise or play sessions. Teach her to recognize the word "outside" by saying it every five seconds or so until you are all the way out of the door. Then take her to a specific area where you want her to eliminate. Use a cue like "Do your business", and gently keep repeating that until she begins to squat and then precisely as she performs, followed by gentle praise; you don't want to distract her with too much praise.

Repeat this process consistently throughout the day. Learn to recognize the body language of the pup that says, "I have to go" (sniffing, whining, restlessness, circling) as well as the language that says, "I'm not finished yet" (continued sniffing and restlessness). Keep a record of when your pup goes and how often. Not all pups will be the same.

See our book *The Art of Raising a Puppy* for more information about house-training, including paper training.

I live in a big city, and my new puppy's vet has said she should have no walking until she's completed her full round of vaccinations—which means several more weeks! I know I'm supposed to "socialize" a puppy with positive exposures to people and other dogs. How do I do that for the next several weeks?

You do need to follow your vet's instructions on this and keep your puppy away from areas frequented by other dogs until he's fully vaccinated. That includes dog parks, runs, and any grassy strips. But you can still safely socialize your pup—and you should. The behavioral consequences of ignoring socialization can be profound and long-lasting.

One creative solution after your pup has eliminated is to put him in a backpack or other carrier that you wear on your front so he can watch all the sights and sounds of the city as you walk. It's also easy to introduce your pup to people from this position.

Take your puppy in the car with you whenever possible. If you have a small enclosed yard or roof space, exercise and train your pup there, and encourage friends to come over and help so that your dog gets used to meeting other people. Look for local puppy kindergartens and puppy training classes that check for vaccinations and allow pups to play with each other. You can even arrange "play dates" with other dogs whose vaccination history you know.

Is it really true that you can't train a puppy till he's six months old?

We understand training in the broadest possible sense, as a life-long process that starts from the day of a pup's birth. Formally or informally, whether you realize it or not, you are always training your dog, and every minute of the day your dog is learning. As such, training goes far beyond obedience exercises, but in whatever form it must always be appropriate to a dog's age. Socializing, grooming, play and preliminary obedience work are appropriate for puppies as young as six weeks old, but more formal exercises—especially those requiring a training collar—would be totally inappropriate at that age; for a residency training program such as ours, it's best to wait until six months. Keep any training sessions fun and upbeat. Also, remember that you can unintentionally "teach" bad behavior by being too permissive early on, so from the start be sure to keep your puppy from jumping up on you, biting and nipping at your hands, or chewing on inappropriate items.

The Basics
Sit ●
Heel ●
Stay ○
Down ●
Come ○

STELLA

Becoming a Dog

Stella, a Cavalier King Charles spaniel, gets the royal treatment: carriage rides, the finest clothing, pampering of the highest order at every turn. But she's been denied the one thing she really needs—the chance to be a dog. Will a change in circumstances give her the opportunity to reclaim her *canininity*—without losing her regal dignity?

Daynia and Paul live in a suburb in upstate New York, in a well-groomed neighborhood of expensive single-family homes with lush green lawns. They have two dogs: Stella, a Cavalier King Charles spaniel, and Zoey, a Pekingese. By all accounts, it's a happy family group.

Their nickname for Stella is "Princess," and they seem to be doing all they can to clothe her in that mantle—literally. You see, Daynia likes to dress Stella in little doggie outfits: stylish sweaters, frilly frocks and coats with cuffs and collars. She's as pretty as a baby doll all in pink, and she clearly doesn't mind all the fussing it takes to slip paws through sleeve holes, button up buttons, and straighten out hemlines. In fact, Stella gives every appearance of being one of those dogs who genuinely enjoys getting dressed to the nines. There's nothing in her expression—as there often is in dogs who get the Fashion Avenue treatment—that suggests she's uncomfortable or, worse yet, humiliated by the whole experience.

Zoey also has her own wardrobe, and can look just as well-heeled when the family goes out for a stroll. Here again, we mean this quite literally, for Stella and Zoey take their neighborhood "walks" in a two-seat baby stroller. Daynia usually does the pushing, and Paul walks along beside. "They look so prim and proper," he comments, and Daynia replies, "Of course they do. They're in their Sunday best."

Come to think of it, "well-heeled" may not be the best turn of phrase to describe these two pampered pooches. When they do get a chance to dismount and stretch their legs, there's no controlling Stella's antics. She knows none of the basic obedience commands formally, has had no leash training, and is unresponsive to her owners' plaintive voices. Zoey is a little more passive, but Stella is off where she wants to be. About the only direction she'll take is the command—well, it's more of a request—to hop back into the stroller, and most of the time she waits to be picked up and repositioned in her rightful place, in front of Zoey.

> "It's proper for a dog to be *walked* on a walk—not pushed in a carriage."
>
> —Brother Christopher

The fact that Stella won't sit or lie down or do any obedience commands consistently hasn't been much of an issue for Paul and Daynia up to now; they put both dogs—Stella in particular—on that pedestal and that's just where they've wanted them and enjoyed having them. In a way that is remarkable, as Stella was purchased from a local pet store, the type of establishment that is often an outlet for puppy mill breeders. Paul and Daynia have been fortunate: The dogs are healthy, neither is aggressive, and the worst one could say is that they're spoiled. But things are about to change.

Daynia is expecting their first child, and with that reality has come the awareness that they've been treating their dogs as small humans. They're beginning to realize that, though they've meant well, this isn't fair to the dogs. Dogs think, act and see the world very differently from humans. For the relationship to flourish, the dog's unique nature needs to be respected. Part of that will involve some real adjustments in the royal treatment. For one thing, it will be the baby who gets stroller rides, not the dogs. (Yes, they will be getting a brand-new stroller, the couple assures us.) And it will be Paul's responsibility to walk the dogs—that is, *really* walk the dogs.

The problem is, Stella is entirely uncomfortable with a leash—she'd much rather don her short pink jacket with matching hat and booties. After all, this is all she knows. And Paul is having no success trying to teach her any basic obedience commands, let alone leash-train her. "It's been a frustrating and humbling experience," he says. "She's really good at ignoring you," Daynia notes.

Zoey is little better but is somewhat more biddable. When the two dogs have a romp in the back yard, Stella is much more rambunctious, playfully going after Zoey and always coming out on top. Zoey is the submissive one, and although both dogs need training, Daynia and Paul have decided to put Stella first, yet again. "We're picking out the problem child here," Paul says. "Hopefully once Stella is trained we'll be able to transfer what we've learned to Zoey."

Stella's Problems

- Uncomfortable with a leash
- Doesn't know any basic obedience commands
- Used to being treated more like a baby than a dog

"Some are born great, some achieve greatness, and some have greatness thrust upon them."

—Shakespeare, *Twelfth Night*

THE PROBLEM

It's easy to peg Stella's basic problem as a lack of training and to assume that obedience drills will set her right. But her resistance to Paul's initial efforts at training is a sign that a pampering problem has created a situation in which Stella is making all the decisions. She has assumed the role of leader because Paul and Daynia have allowed that.

First, we need to be clear that Stella's dominating interactions with the submissive Zoey are not what we're focusing on. It's the very essence of the natural order of things among dogs for one member of the group to take the alpha position. So long as the dominant dog's behavior isn't overly aggressive or physically harmful, there's nothing to change here. Stella is simply the dominant dog in relation to Zoey.

But the way Stella tries to lead in her interactions with Daynia and Paul is another matter altogether. It is not the leadership of one with extreme self-confidence. Rather, it is leadership by default, expressing itself in her failure to respond to even the most preliminary of training and her resistance to all applications of the leash. As we saw with Tessie and will see again with other dogs, Stella's pack includes the human members of her family, Daynia and Paul, and she's lording it over them as well. There's nothing unnatural to her about not listening to orders: She's royalty, after all. Yet curiously, this doesn't translate into brash, self-confident behavior with Paul and Daynia. She simply does whatever suits her fancy since no one has expected anything different from her.

There's an important difference between Stella and Tessie, though, which has to do with how they attained their rank. It's a difference that will have key effects on the whole approach to our training of Stella, and it emphasizes once again the uniqueness of every dog and the importance of relationship in every aspect of obedience work.

As the well-known expression goes, some are born to greatness, some achieve greatness, and some have greatness thrust upon them.

Taking "greatness" here to mean hierarchical superiority—not the true greatness we believe all living creatures are born to—Tessie would fall in the "achieving greatness" category: Through a tussle of wills with her owner, Maude, Tessie lay claim to a dominant position. Stella, on the other hand, clearly has had greatness thrust upon her. She was coddled from her first day with the family and put on that throne through no efforts of her own. There was no storming of Paul and Daynia's family castle—just a fancy, full-dress coronation. It's more as if she said to all of it, "Well, okay," than "Ah, mine. All mine! Off with their heads!"

All playfulness aside, does that really make a difference to the issue of Stella's behavior and how to correct it? To train her effectively, we will still need to turn her world around and show her that humans have to be the leaders. We will need a proper leash and training collar to begin communicating meaningfully with Stella, but even more expansively, we believe strongly in a holistic approach to training, to keeping all aspects of canine personality and the relationship with humans in mind as we go about teaching basic commands. And we do have as our ultimate goal

What They're Thinking

STELLA:
"I'm ready to get down now."

DAYNIA:
"She's our princess."

THE MONKS:
"Stella has never had to obey commands. Now she's being asked to. To her, it's like a palace coup."

enabling the dog to achieve true greatness—which for all of us is about becoming who we really are.

With Stella, then, we will address the leadership problem with a subtly different approach. This will not be so much about unseating her from a position she craves as it will be about helping her occupy one she's never known. Yes, she has accepted her regal role and enjoyed it, but there's another role we're sure she's never had a chance to try and might like even better: the role of being a dog. Our goal will be to let that true nature have an opportunity to emerge and thrive.

We also must address the problem of the kingmakers: Daynia and Paul must adjust their thinking about how they treat their dogs. They clearly now want a dog who will obey commands, and they seem willing to treat her in a new way. But whereas Maude struggled against Tessie's dominance, Daynia and Paul willingly put Stella where she is and enjoyed relating to her in that way. Their struggle may very well be with their own attitude to the human-dog relationship.

AT THE MONASTERY

Stella doesn't live too terribly far from our monastery at New Skete, and Daynia can make the trip easily one morning. Not surprisingly, Stella travels in the lap of luxury, perched on a pink blanket that covers her bed on the passenger seat beside Daynia. "This is it," Daynia says to Stella, who looks back serenely. "This is your big day."

After putting Stella on the ground to stretch her legs and take a potty break, Daynia lifts her back into the car so she can speak undistractedly with Brother Christopher for the initial portion of the entrance interview. For about forty minutes they will discuss Stella's behavior (as well as Paul and Daynia's) and clarify the goals and expectations of the course without Stella's interference. It is important for Brother Christopher to get as clear a sense of what has been going on as

"My prescription for Stella is not to teach her how to be a dog, but to let her be a dog."

—Brother Christopher

possible, as well as reassure Daynia about the value of the training. He knows that Daynia feels a month is a very long stretch.

The time has come for Brother Christopher to meet Stella, and it is interesting that when Daynia goes to get her, she lifts her out of the car—leash dangling from Stella's collar—and carries Stella toward Brother Christopher, placing her at his feet, only to then take up the leash in her hand. It's a subtle thing, certainly, but Daynia's reluctance to walk Stella on the leash, even if only for a short distance, is apparent.

After a few words of greeting while Stella wags her tail happily, Brother Christopher asks Daynia to walk Stella back and forth, just 10 or 20 feet, so he can see how Daynia handles Stella on the leash. The first move Stella makes is to go around behind Brother Christopher's legs, to a position that makes it awkward for Daynia to get things started. It's a funny kind of move for a dog to make with a complete stranger, but we don't read too much into it. Stella just seems to be looking for the most convenient obstacle between herself and any kind of walk on a leash.

They finally make their ambling way along for several paces. Stella neither pulls nor follows Daynia's direction; there's a little bit of this, and a little bit of that, but nothing that comes anywhere close to being purposeful.

Next Daynia tries to make Stella sit. There's no sign of recognition from Stella, and Daynia compounds the problem by repeating the command several times, all to no avail. One of our basic tenets is that you should say commands clearly and firmly and say them only once; repeating a command only teaches the dog to wait for more than one repetition before responding. It's the classic form of unintentionally conditioning a dog to precisely what you don't want them to do.

THE MONKS' WAY

A Touching Encounter

Almost all dogs love to be petted and stroked. But this isn't always a given, and there are some kinds of necessary physical handling that many adult dogs resist if they haven't been properly conditioned.

At New Skete, we begin specialized handling of the puppies from the day they're born. This ensures a well-socialized dog that gives you the best chance of a rock-solid temperament. All of us involved in raising our puppies take part in this handling—"it's a joy for us as well as the pups"—says Brother Stavros. With all the new puppies, Brother Stavros takes time to habituate them to human touch with a thorough, hands-all-over approach, massaging every muscle. "I make sure to work with their feet and their paws," he says, "so that when the time comes to cut their nails, they'll be accepting of that." The same goes for the mouth and ears. Dogs who get this kind of attention right from the start are relaxed and responsive and know to be trusting when they need to be examined. Vets in particular love a New Skete dog!

Brother Christopher, ever looking for something positive to build on, asks if Stella will perhaps instead lie down. Daynia laughs and shakes her head, then half-heartedly tells Stella to lie down. No surprise—nothing doing. Daynia reverts to sit and finally, with the application of a little force to Stella's back end, gets her to assume the position. Less than two seconds later, Stella is up and sniffing at the edge of the path while Brother Christopher says to Daynia, "Okay, I see what we've got here, and it's okay." The issues are clear to Brother Christopher in the behavior of both parties, and his "okay" is to let Daynia know it's nothing new to him, and nothing that can't be fixed. He has Daynia say goodbye to Stella in a somewhat restrained way and then quickly leads the dog to the kennels before we share a few more thoughts with Daynia.

Uneasy lies the head...

Daynia and Paul's pampering of Stella has all been with the best of intentions, and it's obvious that they have treated their dog well—at least in terms of how much attention she gets. We reassure Daynia that we understand these things, and that one could do worse than spoil a dog. But one could also do much better, and we want both her and her husband to understand what may be problematic about all this—besides just the issue at hand of her being untrained and seemingly untrainable.

There's a tendency in people who have dogs like King Charles spaniels to think their regal demeanor—head usually held high, nose tipped up—is a reflection of their inner nature, a breed personality. The owners see their pampering as merely playing to that natural tendency and bringing it out.

In reality, spaniels aren't naturally haughty, superior or prone to a life of leisure. Although the Cavalier King Charles spaniel was indeed bred as a companion for aristocratic types, their forebears were working dogs who made excellent small-game hunters and loved the chase. Today, this breed tends to reveal spirited, happy dogs that adapt well to family life and are good with children. Because they are so notoriously cute, they are easy to spoil, but trainers find them very intelligent. Their ancestral roots, then, predispose them to respond well to training; they love praise and are eager to please.

We have explained to Daynia as tactfully as possible that Stella has become a princess not because she was born to it but because she was raised, by herself and Paul, to it; she responded to the particular kind of attention they lavished on her. And in the process, we believe, they inadvertently denied her the chance to be more what she was bred to be.

And now Stella is getting mixed signals, which can be very confusing and stressful. She cannot be a princess anymore, and she doesn't know how to be a dog. Her owners' frustration with her, unfair though it may be, has led to some noticeable anxiety in Stella, according to Daynia. Recently, she has become more "clingy," less self-assured than in her earlier months. Uneasy indeed may lie the furry head that wears this crown.

We know we can set Stella on the right path, but we also know that she will still crave attention from her owners when she gets back home, and that she will only thrive and grow when she knows she is pleasing them. Our guidance to Daynia is to prepare to lavish a new kind of attention on Stella—an attention that will play to her true canine nature and allow it to emerge.

Stella learning a controlled walk

Brother Christopher begins walking with Stella (1), and when she starts to get ahead he turns in the opposite direction (2), giving a leash pop to get her attention. He steps into the leash and gives an encouraging slap to his thigh, saying "Let's go" (3 and 4). Stella sees Brother Christopher out ahead and falls into line, walking beside him (5 and 6).

STELLA'S TRAINING

Keeping in mind that Stella doesn't have an inherent urge to be dominant and may turn out to be very willing once she understands what is expected of her, we begin her training gently. Especially with dogs who have had little exposure to obedience drills, it pays in the initial sessions not to come on too strong. "I like to establish a context," says Brother Christopher, "from which we can work in a sort of team spirit."

He begins Stella's training in the paved exercise area outside the kennels, and although she's unfamiliar with a training collar and being led around on a leash, she doesn't resist; Brother Christopher's hold on the leash is comfortably firm and communicates his own confidence in the situation. His first words to her are soft but encouraging: "Let's go, Stella." Then they begin walking, and she follows his confident steps,

"With Stella, if you provide
the leadership, she'll follow."

—Brother Christopher

her tail wagging happily. When she tries to head in a slightly different direction, Brother Christopher gives a quick little pop to the leash and says "No," almost half biting off the word but not shouting or sounding angry. Over the course of only 10 or so steps, he may do this three or four times, bringing her back into line. The fact that her tail is still wagging is a very good sign.

Stella knows nothing about heel, so Brother Christopher starts out with a basic pattern that very quickly establishes in Stella's mind that he's the one leading, as in a dance. Working on the grass, he says to her "Heel" and begins walking forward, allowing her to get out in front for the length of the six-foot leash, then reversing direction, turning into the leash and giving it a short pop with the "No"; he bends down a little and gives three little encouraging slaps to his thigh, saying "Let's go" and gently directing Stella to follow him. Every time she gets in the lead, he goes through the same routine. When she turns to follow him, he praises her warmly.

With some dogs, the occasional food reward helps to reinforce the training, but for Stella it's all about praise. She's a glutton for it, and responds enthusiastically. Brother Christopher pitches his voice in a high register as he says, "Atta girl, Stella! Good girl!" The higher, animated tones tend to increase Stella's enthusiasm and serve as her reward; she much prefers them to the lower tones of a corrective "No."

It doesn't really take long at all for Stella to realize it's in her own best interests to go where Brother Christopher leads, and the easiest place from which to do that is right by his side, in the heel position. "It's all geared to making Stella aware of me," Brother Christopher says, and we're pleased to see that she is already focusing her attention on him almost every step of the way.

Over the next several days her training progresses rapidly, and it quickly becomes apparent that Stella is quite bright. She learns to sit, and to stay in place even while Brother Christopher hops up and down trying to distract her. Her hunger for praise and attention is clear in how good she is about maintaining eye contact. With Stella in a sit-stay, Brother Christopher speaks to her encouragingly, "Look here!" and points to his own eyes, and she locks in, waiting for his next command. "She's really very sharp," Brother Christopher notes.

Stella's eagerness to please, which bodes very well for the success of her training, does have one minor drawback. It manifests itself as Brother Christopher moves into teaching her to lie down.

Stella has done a very good job of learning to stay while she's sitting, responding to the "stop sign" gesture of an open-palm hand held in front of her face. But when Brother Christopher shows her how to lie down and then gives the "Stay" command, she rolls over onto her back, ready for a tummy rub. Time and again she does this, and Brother Christopher can't get even a step away from her before he has to correct her position.

It's not entirely clear what's going on in Stella's mind. Rolling over like this is a classic submissive gesture among dogs and their ancestor, the wolf. Is Stella telling Brother Christopher, "I'm all yours"? It's more likely that this reaction comes from Stella's pampered days. When Daynia would dress Stella, she would often hold her in her lap, baby fashion, in order to slip her paws into sleeves. Perhaps this is the closest thing to a "Down" that Stella knows.

Whatever the motivation, it's important to break the pattern without being too heavy-handed, for this is not the type of down-stay we're looking for. But it's proving to be a hard habit to shake, and Stella's progress seems to be faltering. Brother Christopher can't move on to challenging her ability to stay put in the down position because he's continually having to go back to her and physically re-place her right side up. Nevertheless, it's important that he stay patient and creative.

To break the pattern of her down, Brother Christopher opts for changing the venue. They've been working in the paved area, and perhaps Stella's belly is a little sensitive to the cold, damp concrete. They move over to the grass . . . and it does the trick. Brother Christopher gives her the command, motioning dramatically with his hand, sweeping it down to ground level. Stella is riveted to it and her whole body follows the motion as she drops into the down position. Again dramatically, Brother Christopher swings his arm in an arc that ends with his palm right in front of her nose, saying "Stay." And she stays. It's almost as if you can

Remember These Things
- Use high tones when praising.
- Use low tones for correction.
- Reinforce "Stay" by adding distractions.

see the light bulb going on over her head: "Oh! You want me to stay just like this!" It's a magic moment, and repetition drives the lesson home.

Who let the dog out?

After more than two weeks of leash-training and work in the basic obedience commands and, most important of all, being treated in every way, shape and fashion like a dog, Stella is masterful. The best demonstration is how she now performs the down-stay, which was once so problematic.

In one of her last sessions, shortly before Paul and Daynia's pickup appointment to take her home, Brother Christopher gives Stella the down-stay command and then moves away from her. Distractions are an important component of training and help to "proof," or solidify, the dog's understanding of the exercises. Brother Christopher hops up and down, walks around her, steps over her, moves as much as 15 feet away from her, and she never budges. Then he adds more distractions, taking off his work gloves and tossing them one after the other to fall just a couple of feet in front of her. She watches the gloves as they fly through the air, but then she turns back to look at Brother Christopher, who reinforces the stay by saying the command again and giving her the stop-sign gesture with his hand. She doesn't move a muscle . . . except for her enthusiastic tail.

Stella has become a very well-behaved dog. And she clearly loves it.

STELLA TRANSFORMED

Paul and Daynia come together to pick Stella up and spend a good bit of time with Brother Christopher going over the training before they even see Stella. During the time of Stella's training we asked both Daynia and Paul to read our two books so that they would have a basic grounding and could ask meaningful questions at the final demonstration. It's important

Paul walks Stella at heel

This lesson is more for the owner than the dog. Paul gives Stella the heel command and sets out at a brisk pace (1). He turns to the right and starts to come back (2), and Stella stays right beside him through the turn. Note the position of Paul's hands, holding the leash in preparation for giving a corrective pop with his left hand if necessary (3).

for them to first understand the basic obedience exercises conceptually before they try it in real life and to have the freedom to ask questions. Finally, however, the moment to see Stella arrives, and they are astounded at the transformation as they watch from a vantage point where she can't see them. Their little dog who wouldn't obey any commands is going through the full routine of all the basics without a hitch. They notice as well how eagerly she watches Brother Christopher and how happy she seems to be about the whole thing.

"That's not the Stella I remember," Paul says. Is this a sign of trouble, that perhaps he misses his little princess? We think not. Clear in Paul's eyes is how proud he is of her newfound obedience. But will he and Daynia be able to follow through with treating their dog like a dog?

We take a fair amount of time coaching them on our general approach and walking them through the proper techniques for delivering commands. Part of the problem they had with Stella before was their own unfamiliarity with training. So we walk through it all. Paul goes first

and does well, though he needs to work at raising the pitch of his voice when praising. Daynia has a different challenge: After she gets Stella to sit for the first time, she starts praising her and it quickly devolves into a love connection as Stella rolls over for a tummy rub. Brother Christopher kindly but firmly corrects Daynia: "Stella sat; she didn't just win an Olympic medal. Be careful not to overpraise her." The point is that during training sessions like this, a little formality needs to be maintained. There is a time and place for relatively unbridled affection, but training is all about showing leadership and confirming roles: Daynia must be in charge, and Stella must continue to be a well-behaved canine.

We're confident that Stella knows her stuff now, and that she enjoys being allowed to be a dog. But we do have some concerns about Daynia and Paul's ability to change the patterns of their own behavior toward Stella. It's vitally important that they alter their relationship to her—not by paying any less attention to her, but by paying the right kind of attention, the attention that confirms her status as a canine member of the family.

Time will tell, but initially at least all signs are positive. Both Paul and Daynia follow through on training sessions, and they take Stella for leash-walks through the neighborhood. The stroller has been relegated to a storage shed. For Stella, out of sight should keep it—and her old ways—out of mind.

(For a while, they will work with Stella alone; later, now that they know how, they will train Zoey. The two dogs still get along well, their dominant and submissive roles intact, as we fully expected.)

As Daynia's delivery date approaches, Paul takes a more and more active role in Stella's continued training. And the best sign for the future is how he feels about it all. "I see a contentment in her," he says. "I think she looks happier and more content all around."

Their relationship has been transformed. The attention and love is still there, still being lavished, but with a profound difference. Stella is clearly happy to be treated like a dog, and Paul and Daynia are equally pleased to treat her that way.

Q&A: At the Doc's

How do I go about finding a good vet?

First, it's a good idea to seek the recommendations of others you know and trust. Ask your dog-owning friends for referrals, or contact a local kennel or training club or the police department to see which veterinarians they use. Location and convenient office hours will also likely be a factor in your search.

Next, because it's important to have a good relationship with your animal's caregiver, we suggest asking to speak with a prospective veterinarian before bringing your dog for her first visit. Be aware of your own feelings about the conversation: Do you feel comfortable with this person, or do you feel talked down to? Ask to see the facility. This is a reasonable request, and you want to be sure the place is CLEAN (as important in a veterinary hospital as in any medical facility) and well-ordered. Ideally the area for surgeries should be separate from the general treatment room.

Ask whether they use a referral service for particular issues beyond their own expertise or the facility's capabilities. A veterinarian who is humble enough to refer to other colleagues and specialists is valuable. Finally, what are the veterinarian's thoughts about holistic and alternative therapies? While some veterinarians are skeptical of their value, are they at least open to alternative therapies when traditional methods don't work?

What do I need to know about preventive care for my dog, checkups and the like?

You should arrange for a complete physical exam once a year that includes heartworm and lyme tests, as well as other periodic vaccinations, and a stool sample to check for parasites. On the home front, regular grooming is an essential part of caring for your dog. Depending on the breed, coats should be brushed out at least once a week (some every day), and ears and nails should be checked weekly. Also, daily exercise is a vital part of preventive care (see pages 164-165). Remember to check over your dog after exercise, particularly if she has run through cover and woodland. Check between toes, under arms and on the belly for cuts and seeds or other debris that can create sore spots. Also look for any ticks that need removing. Finally, follow proper feeding guidelines for your dog and resist any temptation to overfeed (see pages 114-115). Recent studies have shown that overfed animals live, on average, two years less than lean animals.

My vet has weekday hours. How should I handle an emergency?

Outside of urban areas 24-hour veterinary care is rare. In such cases, many veterinarians have an answering service to deal with emergencies during off-hours. Be sure to check with your veterinarian about this, and ask for a referral to another veterinarian with an answering service if necessary. Keep the emergency number for a 24-hour clinic or other emergency service handy: in your wallet, in the glove compartment of your automobile if you take your dog in the car, on the refrigerator, or wherever you keep a list of emergency numbers. If you have a cell phone, program the number into your list of saved numbers. Because you may be distraught if your dog has been seriously injured, it's also wise to know ahead of time how to get to the emergency clinic; write down the directions or print out a map and keep it where you can easily find it.

I see food products promoted at my vet's office. Does that mean they're good for my dog?

Always be aware that you are the one who is responsible for what you feed your dog, so it's up to you to be as informed as possible about your dog's nutrition (see pages 114-115). Your veterinarian is one good resource in making that choice. Veterinarians often promote certain foods and make them available as a service to their clients, both for convenience and because some dogs will require special foods and diets. There is nothing problematic or unethical about this so long as there's no pressure on you to manipulate your choice. Ultimately, you need to know why you're feeding your dog what you feed. The buck stops with you.

CHICO

Tuning Down an Over-the-Top Dog

This adorable little bundle of love has never really lost his puppy charms—nor his youthful oversupply of exuberance. What's worse, Chico isn't the only miniature poodle bouncing off the walls at home; when he and his partner Jett are together—and that's all the time—chaos rules. Can a dose of discipline cure Chico's excitability and also change the dynamic of two dogs who routinely run riot?

n the world of dogs, it's hard to get much cuter than a pair of minia-ture poodles, one a gorgeous reddish brown, the other a deep, rich black with a blaze of white. But it's also hard to imagine that two such adorable bundles as Chico and Jett could pack so much trouble.

These little whirlwinds of energy live in a comfortably cozy home in one of Washington, D.C.'s urban neighborhoods with their owner, Janell, and her five-year-old son, TJ. Three years ago the family went looking for a poodle puppy and came upon Chico. "He completely took our breath away," says Janell, remembering that love-at-first-sight moment. "He was so darling, a sweet adorable puppy." Jett was in the same kennel with Chico, and Janell just couldn't bear the thought of sep-arating them, they seemed so perfect together. So instead of getting one, she ended up bringing both puppies home—to a household that was already a handful with a two-year-old human toddling around.

They did seem perfect at first, loving and cuddly and calm to boot. Janell was pleased that they seemed particularly relaxed around people. But that didn't last long at all.

Playtime was the first sign of trouble, and a ball was often the cat-alyst. The two puppies fed off each other's energy, ramping each other up, competing for the toy—and soon competing for the humans' atten-tion as well. Adding to the meltdown was the fact that Janell—who had had dogs before, but always adults whom she'd adopted already trained—had no experience dealing with puppies. "I'd been warned about how hard it is to raise two puppies, but I ignored that informa-tion," she recalls. "It was really really difficult."

Janell's busy schedule as a lawyer further complicated things. Realizing she needed help, she hired a professional trainer when the pups were about a year old, and they got two weeks of drilling. The idea was that the trainer would give them each individual attention, teach

"Anybody can train a dog to sit, right?

But not me!"

—Janell

them the basics, and that Janell would then follow through, working with the two of them together. It sounded like a good plan.

But the problem was the follow-through. Janell admits to dropping the ball on practicing daily with Chico and Jett and giving them appropriate attention in the form of regular walks. Like many owners who have hired trainers, she used the excuse that the trainer must have had a magic "something" that the dogs responded to, something she herself just didn't have. That's not our view. When owners accept the discipline of practicing each day with their dog, even for a short fifteen-minute period, day by day things improve. Actually, very few people have an innate, "magical" gift with dogs. Rather, proficiency at handling a dog comes with effort and practice and much of this skill can be learned. But the onus always is on us.

So Chico and Jett never got the chance to cement the lessons they'd learned, and Janell soon discovered that maturity wasn't calming them down any either. She still loved how playful and affectionate they were, but there just seemed to be no "off" button, and it was downright exhausting, each dog competing with the other for Janell's attention.

With no clear, consistent indication of how they should behave, her cute little furballs have become mavens of mayhem. "They're incredibly rude when we have guests," Janell notes, "and I have to put them away in another room until they calm down." She also worries about letting TJ's friends play with them. "They run up and jump on you, trying to get attention, and I'm worried that without meaning to they could hurt one of the kids."

Walks bring out the worst in them. First there's the issue of trying to get the leashes on, with Chico taking the lead in misbehavior. "He goes completely bananas when it's time for a walk," Janell says. "I have to wrestle him to the ground to get the leash on." And it just degenerates from there. When she and TJ try to take them for a walk, the dogs don't get more than a few steps before tangling up each other's leashes. They try to head in opposite directions, pulling and straining, burrowing their little snouts into ivy beds, and not listening to any commands. "Chico pulls to the point of strangling himself," she notes. "I've had to carry him home on occasion because he's so exhausted from pulling."

Especially with Chico, things have gotten to the point that Janell has to some extent given up trying to remedy the situation. Walks are so unpleasant that they now rarely happen. "Because it's so taxing, it makes you *not* want to spend time with him. It's not fun to spend time with a dog who's badly behaved."

Janell knows she needs help and is turning to professionals again. She has chosen to have Chico get the New Skete experience because he's usually the more excitable of the two and, without overly dominating Jett, does seem to hold the top canine position: He has an uncanny knack for getting into the lap first and has laid claim to the prime sleeping territory. Janell's hope is that if Chico can be set right, the overall hysteria level will be significantly lowered and Chico's newfound good behavior will serve as an example for Jett, making him easier for Janell to train herself.

Janell also knows that if the training is to stick, she needs to commit to following through, even given her work schedule, which can have her away up to ten hours a day. "I wish I could snap my fingers and he would be well-behaved," she says, "but I recognize it's going to take a

lot of work and a big commitment on my part. I'm ready to give it a shot—more than a shot. I'm willing to give it a lot of time."

Chico's Problems

- Always wired
- Competing with Jett for attention
- Not obeying any commands
- Pulling on walks, to the point of strangling

THE PROBLEM

Although Chico has had some formal training, it has had little lasting effect because it was never reinforced with consistent practice by Janell. So Chico is for all intents and purposes untrained. But we can also understand why it's been difficult to work with him. He is one extremely excitable dog, always on, loving the spotlight and loving to solicit more and more attention. The fact that there's another dog in the equation only exacerbates this, adding a competitive factor. Couple this with the fact that both dogs lack an appropriate exercise regimen and you have a formula for chaos.

Chico and his family are caught in a bit of a vicious cycle. Chico is so desperate for attention that he becomes a pain about it, which means he's getting less and less play and exercise—which makes him want it all the more and sends him into paroxysms at the slightest hint of an interaction. Janell finds herself yelling at him or telling him to get out of the room when he becomes too crazy. This sends Chico into a sulk, which upsets Janell . . . and on the cycle goes.

What
They're
Thinking

CHICO:
"Yippee! Time for a walk!!!"

JANELL:
"Chico, you're driving me crazy. Calm down!!"

THE MONKS:
"Chico's excitability needs an approach that lowers the hysteria level."

Chico's tendency to become overexcited is also interfering with his ability to learn anything, so that's one phase of his difficulty. But the human side of this relationship needs attention as well. Janell has to be willing to commit time to working with Chico, and with both her dogs. We can guide her on the best approaches to take with an excitable dog, but she must follow through, even if that means including the services of a dog walker to help get the dogs more exercise once they are trained. We do have some concern about her desire for a snap-of-the-fingers solution. Acknowledging the energy she herself will have to invest is the first big step Janell needs to take.

AT THE MONASTERY

Janell has few qualms about leaving Chico at the monastery for four weeks of training. She's so frustrated with him that she makes only passing mention of missing him while he's gone. The positive aspect here is that her eyes are firmly set on the prize. "It will be a dream come true" to have a well-behaved Chico, she imagines. Her only concern is that a transformed Chico might not have the same spirit that—despite all the hassles—she loves so dearly. She doesn't want a robot, even if it does obey all her commands.

On that point we are quickly reassuring. It's clear from our first interactions with Chico on the day he arrives that a broken spirit just will never be part of this dog's future. His personality is way too big for that to be a concern. We emphasize the fact that obedience training is meant to allow a dog's personality to blossom and grow in the context of a right relationship with his owner.

Janell demonstrates for us how difficult Chico is on the leash as she walks around the meeting area with him. She talks about how she can't get him to sit or stay, how he jumps up on people and gets extremely excited. We offer more reassurance, about having seen all this before.

"Chico is bananas, that's the best way to describe him. He is our tornado."

—Janell

And we spend time talking to her about her side of the equation, the time and effort she should expect to contribute to Chico's ongoing training after his time at New Skete.

Chico is, then, a dog who needs a formal program of basic training, first and foremost—no shortcuts. We are confident that our methods will work for him, that his obvious intelligence and eagerness can be turned to the good. Little did we suspect how deeply this little package of energized personality could challenge that confidence.

CHICO'S TRAINING

Day one in the exercise area reveals to Brother Christopher that Chico is completely unfamiliar with a training collar and with any kind of leash correction. As they go through the heel drill—which Brother Christopher typically uses as an evaluation of the dog's level of training—Chico yelps at the least little corrective pop on the leash. He is extremely excitable, and won't hold any of the basic positions. Brother Christopher uses all his customary techniques for getting Chico into the sit position, but he won't hold it for even a couple of seconds. He bounces and jumps and yaps, as if to say, "Look at me!" as Brother Christopher tries to focus his attention on the command to sit.

And then Chico starts to exhibit an unusual behavior, licking around his own muzzle very rapidly and obsessively, his tongue flicking in and out almost as if he'd eaten peanut butter. It's not something Janell has mentioned, and it's enough of a concern that we arrange a visit to the vet, just to make sure nothing is wrong. He gets a thorough check—and a clean bill of health. There's nothing medically wrong to account for the licking behavior, although it could perhaps be a response to a minor nasal irritation. However, the most probable explanation is stress: Despite the fact that he is already three years of age, this is the first time that Chico has ever been away from home and the first time he has ever been separated from Jett. With other dogs periodically barking in the kennel and setting him off, Chico's first days at New Skete have upped the ordinary amplitude and made things difficult.

Brother Christopher is finding himself challenged by Chico's failure to make any progress during these first days, and starts asking himself questions that have an edge of worry to them. "Am I going to be able to help this dog? Why is it taking so long for him to get this? What am I going to do to turn this around?"

Few of us are unfamiliar with the moment of doubt; it seems to be a natural attribute of our human condition. What we at New Skete strive for, though, is to replace those stagnant pools of doubt we wallow in with clear, renewing streams of faith and confidence that move us on. Doing so is, in part, a process of refocusing attention away from self and toward the relationship at hand, toward the act of coming into an enriching relationship with another living being.

Since each dog is unique, trainers need to be flexible with how they approach training. Training is not really a "one size fits all" profession. Thinking is required, and the trainer who stubbornly holds on to his or her "method," come hell or high water, will inevitably find some dogs doing poorly, never approaching what their real capacities are. After moments of reflection, Brother Christopher decides to focus his own attention on his deep-seated belief in the training process, and to project that quiet confidence into all his interactions with Chico. It may be that Chico has been picking up on his anxiety "vibes," and that this, combined with Chico's own nervousness, has been helping to interfere with Chico's ability to learn the commands. So Brother Christopher tells himself to "believe in the process, simply and calmly believe in the process—and in the dog."

Chico faces distraction

Brother Christopher puts Chico into a sit and tells him to stay (1). A helper brings distraction in the form of Harley, and Chico responds by breaking the sit-stay (2). Brother Christopher gives a leash pop and verbal correction, and puts Chico back into the sit-stay, making sure Chico's paying attention to him (3). Chico gets the point and doesn't break when Harley comes by again (4).

"When challenged with a dog like Chico,
I remind myself to believe in the process,
simply and calmly believe in the process—
and believe in the dog."

—Brother Christopher

Looking anew, then, at the dog before him, Brother Christopher sees an aspect of his state of mind that needs direct addressing. Chico is unsure of the whole situation he's in; that alone is not so unusual, especially with a dog who has never been kenneled before. But Chico is unsure in other, more fundamental ways. He doesn't know what's required of him, what the expectations are, and this is something that has been happening over a length of time. In a largely directionless environment, his confidence in himself has been steadily eroded. Not deliberately, of course. In fact, you might think from the looks of things that Chico has been brimming over with confidence, knowing what he wants and doing all he can to get it, and that the problem at home is that Janell just hasn't known how to rein it in. But Chico's demonstrative behavior, his straining on the leash, all his high-strung ways are much more likely his almost fevered response to not knowing what's really expected — what he needs to do to be the good dog who deserves the spotlight of attention he loves so much.

In this context, it's more obvious that Chico's unusual tongue flicking behavior is a sign of nervousness and uncertainty. He often goes into it after being given a command, almost as if he's sitting there saying, "Is this what you want? I'm not sure and, and, and, I'm nervous I'm not getting it right!" You can almost feel the tornado of excitability winding up.

So Brother Christopher decides, first, to project confidence, and then to take steps to keep Chico's emotional volatility in check. He reminds himself not to worry that the training is taking longer than he'd like, to realize it will likely be a process of gradually building up Chico's self-confidence to a point where he trusts his own sense of what the expectations are as that is combined with the training. From there, his willingness — indeed, his all-too-evident eagerness — can become a constructive, rather than destructive, force in his training.

THE MONKS' WAY

That Something Special

Many owners imagine that trainers such as ourselves have some special something about us that dogs respond to. We do feel we have something special, but it's not an innate attribute, not some magic, charismatic touch. Anyone can learn it.

What we have is an attitude of paying attention to the reality before us, and doing so dispassionately but not disinterestedly. What does that mean? It means that we try never to just go through the motions of a training technique, even when it's one that we know almost always works. In every action, every command, we concentrate on maintaining our awareness. Is the dog responding? How quick is my correction and is it of an appropriate level of force? Is repeating this command going to give it another chance to work—or is it going to risk reinforcing the unwanted behavior? What else might be going on in this dog's mind? Is he afraid, or distracted, or tired? Am I getting frustrated?

Asking ourselves these questions helps to keep us focused in a holistic way on everything that may be influencing the training situation, including our own reactions and attitudes. And it keeps us calm and confident, reminding us that—even when nothing seems to be working—there is always a way, and we can find it.

The Rule of Calm

Many dogs need animated encouragement to obey commands. It's typically the case that we have to praise dogs, effusively at first, to communicate the notion that obeying commands is a good and fun thing. But in Chico's case, animation is the last thing he needs. So Brother Christopher's training sessions with him are exercises in calm—calm tones, almost no tactile attention in the form of petting or stroking, no encouraging rapid slaps on the thigh to focus his attention. They walk around the exercise area quickly, Brother Christopher correcting any straying or pulling with gentle leash pops, but ones that are carefully administered so as not to wind Chico up in any way. "I need to be constantly aware not to overdo the leash correction," he says, "but not to let him control the situation either."

Chico is learning that there's a time
for exuberance, and a time to follow direction.

It's certainly challenging, but a few things help. It's of course vital that Chico learn to pay attention to the human at the other end of the leash, and one way Brother Christopher accomplishes this while keeping things low-key is by varying the pace at which he walks. It's more effective with Chico than the sudden change of direction that is usually the failsafe method of focusing the untrained dog. Without getting riled up, Chico starts to understand that he needs to watch Brother Christopher's steps carefully to keep things moving smoothly. Interestingly, as the pace slows down Chico idles down as well, and he begins to visibly relax into the heel.

The Importance of Recess

But even more important for Chico's progress is lots and lots and lots of exercise. His training begins to make the most progress after he's had a chance to burn off some of his energy first, whether in a long walk or vigorous, unstructured playtime. He absolutely loves chasing a tennis ball back and forth or playing with any kind of toy, and it does wonders by giving him an outlet for his excitability.

Studies have shown that children's learning suffers when they don't get time for recess, and the same thing holds true for our little friend Chico. There's no question that he loves playing, that it's something he's been missing, and that he learns better afterward. There may be a double benefit at work. The exercise and play lower his overall energy level, but they also may be helping him disassociate training from excitability. He's learning that there's a time for exuberance, and a time to follow direction.

WHAT IF tip

If your dog gets overly excited at the mention of a walk, turn to an obedience command. Use the sit command before going through the door on any occasion, even if it's not for a walk. Habituate your dog to sitting before you start a play session, introduce a stranger, or put down the food dish. You reinforce your leadership and confirm that anything good or fun requires some obedience first.

CHICO'S PROGRESS

After two weeks, Chico is doing better and better. He has learned to sit and hold it for a longer and longer time. An interesting observation in this regard is that the use of a treat actually got in the way of Chico's learning. Like a little circus dog he would immediately break whatever he was doing as soon as the reinforcement was given: hopping up on his legs, for example, after a sit. Quiet, warm praise seemed to work much better, keeping Chico more focused on Brother Christopher and more relaxed in holding the command.

> "There's been a certain joy I've seen in him that has made me feel very good."
>
> —Brother Christopher

On the stay command, he is at first sensitive to Brother Christopher walking around behind him; he turns his head nervously and it often breaks him from the stay. So Brother Christopher keeps the leash a little bit taut, holding it straight up even as he circles around Chico, and this helps keep him in place while he gets used to the general idea of the human walking around while the canine stays put. Over the course of several days' worth of training sessions, Chico visibly relaxes as not only Brother Christopher but also his assistant Janine and a variety of other dogs walk around him in a circle. His intelligence has caught up with his emotions and his tongue flicking is becoming much less frequent.

With each little success, Chico seems to be gaining in self-confidence. This is certainly in part because his training sessions are consistent both in frequency and in the content of what he's asked to do. The repetition is helping him to relax, and his more relaxed attitude is making it easier for him to learn. He's happy without going over the top.

As his training time nears an end, he shows even more success. In

training with another dog, he holds to a stay or doesn't break heel as the two dogs go past each other in opposite directions. Brother Christopher can toss distractions his way, and this dog who loves to play with toys – stuffed toys, balls, sticks – stays put because he's been given that command. One of the surest signs of his more focused nature is that he isn't even disturbed by the presence of a film crew that is shooting some video of our training techniques. This is quite an accomplishment for Mr. Spotlight. That spotlight is literally right there, and Chico behaves where once he would have been bouncing and spinning away in his "Look at me!" mode.

Brother Christopher is particularly gratified with the fundamental security he sees radiating from this still-energetic animal. "The special thing I see with Chico," he says, "is the part of him that has been unlocked during play. He hasn't had the opportunity to express that because in the past he was so uncontrollable. But now there's been a certain joy I've seen in him that has made me feel very good, particularly given the challenges I experienced at the beginning of the training."

CHICO TRANSFORMED

Janell comes to pick up Chico, and Brother Christopher shows off his ability to walk calmly at heel and to sit on command, without repeated prompting or the physical "assistance" in the form of a push down on the butt that Janell had so often resorted to. He also holds a stay when Brother Christopher lightly holds the leash and walks all around him. Most impressive of all, Chico seems happy and sure of what's going on without getting too exuberant. He goes through all of the remaining commands without difficulty and preserves his focus.

Any concerns Janell might still harbor that her dog has been turned into an automaton are wiped away when she comes outside to meet him. There he is, all over her, pure joy in greeting. After allowing a few moments of unfettered response, Brother Christopher guides Janell into giving Chico the round of commands he's best at. And he falls into line. The exuberance is, if not put aside, held in abeyance. But it certainly hasn't been snuffed out.

Chico is, at this point, sure of himself and of what the expectations are, and his enthusiasm never spills over into chaotic activity. But will it stick? Will he hold to what he's learned—and hold onto his confidence—when he gets back with Jett? Or will the competition between the two take center stage again and cause things to spin out of control?

It all depends now on Janell. We stress again to her how important both routine exercise and consistent obedience training are for the very high-strung, excitable dog. When it's time for training, she will have to provide a foundation of her own calm confidence to control and focus Chico's attention. But at the same time she will have to be sure that Chico is in an emotional equilibrium that will enable him to learn. And that means he needs regular exercise and a consistent structure of both play and training on a daily basis. In fact, we tell her, if both dogs are to learn and progress together, she will need to find a way to give each of

them their own, uncompetitive space. There will need to be playtimes that are just for Chico, and others that are just for Jett. Each dog will need to have moments of attention that are solely for that dog. Janell needs to build in them the confidence that they don't need to compete for her attention or affection.

Finally, we also want Janell to acknowledge to herself that her own schedule and the demands she faces on her time are real challenges she must be aware of. She may have a tendency to say on occasion, I'll let it pass today. We want her to remember in those moments that she risks going back to the chaos.

But we also hold out the very real hope of further joys ahead with the proper investment of attention. Indeed, when Janell hosts the film crew for a follow-up several weeks after returning home, the change from before is obvious. It is clear Janell has been following through and Chico is all the better for it. In fact, the lessons have begun to transfer over to Jett as well, and both dogs have learned to walk on heel together with a single leash and a y-shaped coupler. The change from before is remarkable. Going to the park to exercise the dogs and to play with TJ is no longer a source of frustration but something to look forward to. Yet this still is but a start. The best thing for Chico—and for Jett—will be ongoing opportunities for learning. By challenging her dogs in healthy ways, Janell can ensure that they will become ever more attuned to her expectations—and thus calmer and more confident. The payoff—well worth what it will take to accomplish—will be not only a more serene house but also deeper, more rewarding bonds among them all.

Q&A:

Feeding More than the Soul

I want to do best by my dog, but some of the organic foods are more expensive and I don't know if it's worth it. What's the best, least expensive nutritional plan for my dog?

It's best not to even think in terms of least expensive—or most expensive, for that matter. Your dog's health, behavior and longevity are intimately linked to the food you use, so think in terms of its quality rather than its cost. Be as responsible and informed as possible about what you're feeding your dog. Consult your breeder or veterinarian, both of whom know your dog firsthand. You can also get valuable information from magazines and the Internet—but beware of Web sites that are basically glorified advertisements for specific brands.

From your research you will undoubtedly learn that dogs need a balanced diet, so be sure to look carefully at food labels. As carnivores, dogs need meat, so choose a food in which animal proteins are two of the first three ingredients. Dogs also need some carbohydrates in the form of grains and vegetables. Oats, barley and brown rice are grains that contain lots of vitamins and minerals. Avoid products with corn and soy, which are difficult for dogs to digest. We recommend foods preserved naturally with vitamins C or E, and we stay away from those preserved artificially. Consider adding a nutritional supplement to your dog's food to compensate for nutrition lost in the baking process.

Ultimately, however, how your dog does on the food is key. Look for palatability, glossy coat, non-itchy skin, firm stools and bright eyes.

I'm worried about recent scares on food content and health problems— even deaths—in dogs. What do I need to watch out for?

The pet food recalls of March 2007 illustrate the challenge of feeding your dog safely. In an increasingly global economy where food ingredients come from a variety of sources, some of which may have less-than-stellar quality standards, we advise being thorough in your understanding of what your dog is eating. A quick check of the FDA and American Veterinary Medical Association Web sites (www.fda.gov and www.avma.org) will give you peace of mind about the food you're giving your dog, especially if you're switching brands or hear something on the news about a recall.

If you have really lost faith in commercial preparations, you can always go to a home-prepared diet, but be aware that you'll need to do serious research to make sure your dog is getting all the ingredients he needs in correct proportions. Home-prepared diets are not for owners looking for convenience. You have to be responsible, consistent, and willing to take the time to do it properly— no filling the dish with whatever leftovers and table scraps are available.

My dog is so finicky, and often doesn't eat what we give him. We've tried multiple brands and combinations of wet, dry or both, and still he's picky. What do we do now?

If your dog suddenly becomes finicky, there might be a medical reason—bad teeth or a throat infection, for example, so first check with your vet. If this is an ongoing thing, though, and you've already gotten into the habit of trying different brands to please a fussy palate, you're actually just making matters worse. Soon you'll be feeding him caviar! To regularize his diet, pick a good food and stick with it. Give him fifteen minutes to eat and feed him in his crate or some private area away from distractions. If he doesn't eat, pick the food up and do not offer it to him again until the next mealtime. Discontinue any treats, and follow the same procedure at the next meal. Trust us, no healthy dog will starve himself. Keep to this rhythm and when your dog gets hungry enough he will eat, and learn to eat right away.

Let your dog's weight and condition be your guide to his need for food. Don't worry if your dog doesn't eat even if it's for several days. Sometimes this happens—as with an unneutered male dog when a female in heat is nearby. If your dog is drinking and his weight looks good, be patient and don't feel guilty. He'll eat.

The Basics
Sit ○
Heel ●
Stay ○
Down ○
Come ●

HOLLY

A New Leash on Liveliness

Meet Holly for the first time indoors, and you'll be charmed both by her elegant looks and by her intelligent, friendly nature. In an undistracted situation she demonstrates the training her dog-savvy owners have given her. But see her outside near the street and you'll more likely be horrified by her lunging, leg-entangling—and potentially downright lethal— antics. This standard poodle lives by a double standard when it comes to obedience. Her owners are perplexed and find her just plain too hard to handle at times. They need help.

Bruce and Carolyn have a down-to-earth quality about them that fits well in the serene little town of Cambridge, New York, where Bruce serves as pastor of the Presbyterian church. We know Cambridge well—it's just down the road from New Skete—and we can't help but feel a natural bond with our close neighbors. So we are particularly drawn to help these folks with a difficult situation that involves their adored—but sometimes less than adorable—standard poodle, Holly. Both Bruce and Carolyn have had knee replacement surgery, which makes it hard for them to be as mobile as they'd like to be. And that has affected their relationship with their rather boisterous dog.

To be fair, Holly isn't always a handful. In fact, there are times in the house when she is well-behaved and charming. But get her riled up during an indoor play session, or excited when bikes and cars pass by the front window, and the picture changes dramatically. Holly becomes very difficult to manage. Bright-eyed and curious from the day they got her— "she poked her head out of the blanket we had her wrapped in for the car ride home, looking at everything around her," Bruce remembers— Holly began playing indoor games when she was still a young puppy. "We called her the cruise director," Carolyn says, because *she* would be the one to decide which toy was getting played with, and which of the two humans would be allowed to play. As she grew older, she became really good at selectively following commands to fetch and bring back the plaything, or to sit and wait for a couple of seconds first.

"Holly knows her own mind—and I'm losing mine."

—Carolyn

"She always sits on command," notes Carolyn, "or even initially on her own before I put her food down." Truth be told, there's nothing more endearing than a dog who waits patiently for food—wouldn't even think of begging—and who, again assuming there are no distractions present, seems to be reading your mind when it comes to obeying commands. Poodles, which many people claim are the most intelligent of all dogs, are known for showing off in this way, and for making up their own tricks to impress their owners. Holly clearly got her own dose of poodle smarts—and sweetness as well. Curled up at her owners' feet, or rolling over for a tummy rub, Holly only seems to be adding to the serenity and groundedness that envelop this happy home.

There's even one more impressive entry on the plus side of the ledger. When it's time to go out, Holly sits at the door, waiting for Carolyn or Bruce to precede her—stellar behavior that we often recommend as one of the most important ways to teach a dog about leadership and "pack" authority. Holly's already got it down pat.

But there's obviously another Holly waiting in the wings, and as soon as you step out that door, the other Holly makes her entrance. Quite an entrance it can be.

"When we take her for a walk," Bruce says, "she almost always runs around in zigzags and circles, and she's happy to do that—especially when she can wrap the leash around one or both of us." That's not exactly her motivation. What's really going on is that Holly is in the mood to play. And as Bruce notes with a wry smile, "her favorite toys in the yard are large trucks and school buses. She loves to chase them." She doesn't really get the chance—her owners never let Holly run loose—but she certainly makes the effort, barking away, bucking and lunging against the restraint of the leash, and arcing back and forth as she follows each vehicle zooming along the nearby road.

"Easy does it, easy does it, girl," Bruce says over and over again as Holly goes ballistic at the end of the retractable leash they use with her. Carolyn prefers the retractable leash because she feels it allows her to compensate for Holly's lunging by letting the leash out a little. But when used as a substitute for formal training on a normal six-foot leash, it loses its value and proves totally ineffective as a tool of communication. Worse, it can be dangerous. If a dog happens to pull the handle out of the owner's hands from a sudden lunge, it can easily scare a dog as the handle retracts wildly toward the dog. This can cause the dog to bolt away in fear. It also leads to those entanglements that have already put

Holly's Problems

- Entangling people in the leash
- Lunging at vehicles
- Failing to obey any commands when she's distracted

HOLLY:
"Car! Truck!! School bus!!! PLAY!!!!"

BRUCE AND CAROLYN:
"She's out of control and won't listen!"

THE MONKS:
"Yes, she's out of control—she is
not being properly leash-controlled."

a scare into her family more than once. Bruce fell one time because of Holly's pulling and twisting; only the fact that there was a lot of snow on the ground prevented him from being injured.

Bruce and Carolyn are also of course worried that Holly will get loose and run out into the road, or maybe even hurt someone else as she jumps and bounces around. Their problem is that they can't find a way to get her to obey them when she carries on like this. Holly ignores their verbal entreaties, and the obedience she demonstrates indoors seems suddenly inaccessible. Bruce's "easy does it" has no effect, nor do any of the hand gestures to "stop" or "stay" that can work well inside. Holly—who had problems in a group obedience class because she wanted to play too much—has other things on her mind.

"I want to be able to count on her responding when I really need her to," Carolyn says. "I want her to be safe, and I want us to be safe."

THE PROBLEM

When a dog's misbehavior stems from a specific stimulus—like passing traffic—one might be tempted to focus on that stimulus in the search for answers. With Holly, for example, one might want to investigate what it is about moving vehicles that flips her switch. Was she traumatized by a car at some point in her formative years? Might the roar of the engine heard by her be interpreted as the vocalization of some hostile canine competitor? Nothing that Bruce and Carolyn expressed about her past suggested that. More likely it is simply a domestic expression of Holly's innate prey drive, what evolution has provided canines with to survive on their own.

Whatever the true reasons may be, they have little practical value. Yes, we need to think about underlying motivations, but we don't have to get too Freudian about it, delving into some presumed subconscious conflict desperately conniving to express itself. If you believe in a philosophy of addressing problems holistically, with an eye to the entire life of the dog and her relationship with her owners, that doesn't mean you have to dig deep. All you really need to do is look at the dog's basic needs and the basic circumstances of the dog's life—and what will help to put things right between the two.

We don't need to dig too deep at all to make a good guess at what's affecting Holly's behavior. Hers is a classic case of the underexercised, undercontrolled dog. Without a serious, formal foundation in basic obedience, no amount of wishing, cajoling or bribing will change Holly's behavior. She needs to perceive Bruce and Carolyn as leaders she recognizes and respects.

This being the case, two things immediately stand out as going wrong for Holly in her world. First of all, she isn't getting enough exercise. Her lunging at vehicles isn't so much about the vehicles as it is about expending energy. As we will discover when we get to know Holly better during her first days at the monastery, she launches herself at all sorts of "targets": trucks, cars and buses—but also bicyclists and pedestrians and neighbor dogs and rolled newspapers just picked up from the driveway and any accessible stretch of her own leash, and so on and so on. In other words, Holly sees the outside world as a big bunch of toys that she wants to play with and isn't getting a chance to. She's happy to bound after her soft rubber ball across ten or so feet of open floor in the living room, but what she really wants—and needs—is to stretch her legs in a full-throttle dash outside. So as soon as she sees the open space, and a wide choice of targets, she's off to the races.

What does it really mean that Holly chooses the toy—and the participants—for inside games? It means that she's making too many of the decisions without reference to and proper respect for her owners.

That's problem number one: Holly wants and needs to expend more energy. She is simply not getting adequate exercise because Bruce and Carolyn are afraid of letting Holly run free without a reliable recall. Problem number two is just as significant: Holly's owners aren't handling her properly on the leash. Carolyn uses the retractable leash because it helps her keep her balance, but it's not helping to control Holly outdoors. As we've said, retractable leashes were never meant to make basic obedience training unnecessary. They were meant to give dogs a bit more freedom outside of formal training while still being under control. Further, the give on a retractable leash is a fundamental lesson in *not* having to respond to direction. Instead of getting an immediate, attention-getting correction, Holly gets "give" when she lunges, and she learns from it. Her mad dash at a passing dump truck ends up

Conditioned to Distraction

All dogs are curious about the world around them, but if they haven't been properly conditioned as puppies, curiosities in their environment can easily become distractions that interfere with obedience.

Our New Skete puppies learn early on what to pay attention to and what to ignore. We expose them to a variety of objects and noises—hand clapping, whistling, jangling bells, and thrown gloves, hats or toys. With positive reinforcement, they learn to follow the encouraging clapping of hands as we run with them in a field. But we also teach them to sit quietly and attentively even if a toy goes flying by, or if we're whistling away in a manner that might cause an untrained dog to jump up. And we work to inure them to loud, sudden noises, which agitate many adult dogs who haven't had this kind of conditioning. A metal dish dropped on a concrete floor in the kennel makes a horrific noise, and the puppies at first shy away. But with repeated exposure to the sound, they learn to ignore it. As grown-up dogs, they will never have trouble with thunderstorms or fireworks—or the sudden roar of a passing truck.

giving her more length on the leash, and she doesn't associate the subsequent strain when Carolyn or Bruce reels her in as corrective. She just knows that if she lunges again, she'll maybe get a little more room to operate.

Leash control is something Bruce and Carolyn have already realized they need to work at, but they're somewhat puzzled at Holly's inconsistency. Why is she able to behave periodically indoors, only to morph into an unruly pet at other times, especially when there are distractions present, especially outside?

Looking at the fundamentals pays off again. It tells us that Holly's good behavior inside needs a little interpretation. When she "does as she's told" inside, we need to keep our eye on what is really happening: With nothing competing for her attention, she can obey with nothing to lose.

It's cute, and impressive, but what does it really mean that Holly chooses the toy—and the participants—for inside games? It means that she's making too many of the decisions without reference to and proper respect for her owners. Holly's good behavior—whether it's sitting to wait for the food bowl, or waiting at the front door for a walk, or retrieving and dropping a thrown toy—has a large degree of self-interest in it. While there's nothing inherently wrong with that, it also doesn't mean the good training her owners have given her is dependable in all circumstances. Good solid training has to be absolute, reliable, and never-failing. Holly isn't quite there yet.

We will thus need to work on establishing a relationship of benevolent leadership with Holly and accustoming her to formal training with a proper leash, the focus of which is the basic obedience exercises. And we will need to be creative about finding ways to ensure that her owners give her the exercise she needs without taxing them too much.

AT THE MONASTERY

It's a short ride for Bruce and Carolyn to bring Holly to us at New Skete. She enjoys the trip, as she does any journey in the car; she looks out the whole time, watching everything that's going on. And she's on her very best behavior when she first meets Brother Christopher, lying down in front of him as he hunkers down to greet her. She's a beautiful dog, and her intelligence shines through.

But then Bruce takes her for a "walk" around the meeting area, and it's immediately obvious how poorly leash-trained she is. With the retractable leash locked short, she strains to get at anything nearby, acrobatically going several paces just on her hind legs, her head swiveling back and forth as she checks everything out. Carolyn takes her turn, and as is her custom she lets the leash out more, but amidst such distractions Holly is totally unresponsive to her commands. Within moments, Holly has passed around behind their backs and exhibited her skills at hog-tying her owners. Bruce is carrying her blanket and Holly jumps up trying to grab it. Brother Christopher moves his hand back and forth near her, and she makes a move for that as well.

So it's clear that Holly's interest is in any moving object, not just cars and trucks. She's curious about everything, and distracted by it all as well. Brother Christopher can also see firsthand that her owners need training in how to handle a leash.

Before they leave, we discuss the approaches we'll be taking with Holly. We emphasize that both she and Bruce and Carolyn will need to learn to accept some realities about each other. Indoor play isn't giving

Holly the exercise she needs—exercise that will help transform her erratic ways into more controlled behavior—and it reinforces the perception that she can roughhouse inside whenever it suits her fancy. So we will be looking for methods that will enable them to work her more. At the same time, Holly will need to be trained to their pace; she isn't going to be getting any jogging walks or three-mile excursions from either of her owners.

With dogs, it's almost always possible to make these adjustments. Yes, they are creatures of habit, with specific traits bred into them. But they are also flexible beings, highly intelligent and capable of adapting to a wide variety of circumstances. They would never have gone from wild pack animals to companions of early humans if they didn't have this quality. In fact, experts suggest that domestication was as much a decision of the wolf/dog as it was of human beings. From the standpoint of survival, it was in their interest to associate with human beings.

Finally, we give Bruce and Carolyn some idea of the extra benefits of a well-trained Holly. It's not just that they will be able to control her lunging. As Brother Christopher puts it, "By teaching a dog the formal exercises of basic obedience, you're doing far more than teaching simple tricks. Rather you're giving the dog the capacity to be part of your life in a nonchaotic, natural way. The goal of obedience training is to allow the relationship to blossom organically, by motivating the dog to respond to the owner's commands willingly."

HOLLY'S TRAINING

Predictably, in her first formal training sessions Holly attempts to challenge Brother Christopher's leadership. Since her primary experience to date has been to do what she pleases on the flexi-lead, she repeats that, only now the leash is much shorter. Everything is new to her, and her innate curiosity drives her to bound and lunge and strain against

Indicating "Stay"

Brother Christopher gets Holly to sit (1) and then brings his open palm right in front of her nose as he says "Stay" (2).

the unfamiliar training leash. But there's more going on here as well. You might call it the bad side of her smarts. "Holly definitely has a mischievous character," Brother Christopher notes. "You sense that she's always looking for your weak spots." With Bruce and Carolyn it was going around behind them and wrapping them up in the extended part of her retractable leash. That's not going to work with Brother Christopher, who's using a six-foot training leash attached to a training collar and quickly brings her under control through several quick leash pops coupled with quick changes of direction. So she tries something else, playfully pushing up against him and continually bouncing up. It's another of those games she makes up to try to control the situation. We will be giving her plenty of time to play, but at this early stage, we feel it's best to curtail this behavior as well.

Brother Christopher has experienced this with many dogs, and he soon has Holly focusing on the task at hand. "Heel" is the foundational, primary lesson she really needs to learn. It will ultimately make her controllable when Bruce and Carolyn walk her, but more immediately to the point, it teaches her about who the leader is.

Brother Christopher uses a classic two-step correction to get Holly used to heeling. The purpose is attention-getting, not punitive. When walking, Holly doesn't so much wander off as try to bound as she walks along. When she does so, Brother Christopher gives a quick pop to the leash—that's step one—and then he promptly turns and walks in the opposite direction, encouraging Holly with high-toned praise. It's important to note again that the leash pop doesn't hurt Holly; with her training collar properly in place, high on her neck just behind her ears, the pop merely gets her attention. And with her attention focused, the next thing she sees is Brother Christopher out in front of her—leading the way, encouraging her to follow as he taps his thigh.

This is the exact opposite of what she's been used to with the retractable leash, which always allowed her to be out in front. To get her back close, Carolyn would do her mightiest to reel in the line, and Holly would be at her cleverest finding ways to get Carolyn and Bruce wrapped up first.

But now she's experiencing a leader, and her brains tell her this guy is in charge. She soon is following willingly at Brother Christopher's side, looking up at him and gaiting in a happy prance. She's willing to learn the lesson in part because she's getting lots of chances to practice—and that's giving her exercise she really enjoys. Following the leader, though it may not be her own idea, is an activity she gets into.

Setting the Pace

With each session, Holly is getting better and better at heeling. She likes to please, and Brother Christopher rewards her with praise every time she gets it right. He also incorporates the sit and stay into the routine and Holly catches on very quickly. Simply passing his hand from lower to higher in Holly's path as they heel he says "Sit" simultaneously, and

Holly flows into a sit. She also holds the stay when given the hand command in front of her face. Basic obedience is sinking in with this dog, so now it's time to start fine-tuning her training for the circumstances of her life at home.

"Pace communicates leadership in a very humane, gentle way."

—Brother Christopher

Because both Bruce and Carolyn can't move fast, Brother Christopher starts walking Holly at a slower pace. Brisk heel lessons were important at first, to keep her engaged. But now she needs to learn to adapt. "Pace is an important component of good training," Brother Christopher notes. "It communicates leadership and authority in a very humane, gentle way." To reinforce the lesson—and his own authority—Brother Christopher alters between a crisp, quick pace and the slower gait Holly will have to follow with her owners. Any sign of hesitancy or tentativeness on the handler's part will be exploited by Holly, so he works hard to keep her focus. He is teaching her that everything she wants in the way of a walk is contingent on following the pace being set for her by the leader.

Testing the Road Warrior

Holly has learned heel very well and to adjust her pace. But it would be wrong to think that her newfound obedience will hold sway in the face of the old temptations. Holly's lunging at vehicles, although it was more about wanting to play than anything else, had become a habituated behavior, and we expect that without more work, traffic will still cue an automatic lunging response. So out to a nearby road Brother Christopher takes her—to introduce distraction and unhabituate that ingrained reaction.

Sure enough, as cars go by on a busy stretch of road, Holly tries to get at them. But Brother Christopher is right there, keeping her close by his side and correcting any move she makes with a sharp "No" and a leash pop. Holly will be walking along at heel and hear a car coming from behind, and right away her head swivels. She gets a correction for this as well, and then another – anytime she continues to show interest. It's tough competition, but Brother Christopher needs her to keep her focus on him. Her life may very well depend on it.

Sometimes the temptation just seems too much. When a big truck roars by, Holly lunges up barking. Brother Christopher is particularly firm, giving a very sharp verbal correction and popping the leash strongly to put her into a sit. "She needs to understand that that's absolutely taboo," he says. "I realize that some people feel sharp corrections are totally inappropriate in training, that they are 'mean.' However, if they teach the dog to stay focused on the handler and to ignore distractions that put them at risk, then I'll let the results speak for themselves."

And she does learn, after many sessions walking along the road. Because Holly is so inherently curious and full of energy, she will always have to be at a close heel when she's near a busy road. But the significant triumph is that now she responds to the commands she's given even in the face of the most tempting of distractions.

A New Ball Game

There is one more lesson for Holly, and its goal is to get her the energy discharge that will make her a better-behaved dog in all circumstances,

Holly learns to play ball

Holly goes in full-burst pursuit of a ball (1). She fails to come right back to Brother Christopher, so he steps on the leash to keep her from going off (2); he can then pick up the leash and give her a correction. After she learns the lesson, she gets the ball and heads back (3), returning right to Brother Christopher (4).

even in the face of distractions. Holly needs to learn a new ball game.

Working with a very long 50-foot leash, Brother Christopher starts playing ball with Holly outside. This isn't something she's used to, and at first she tries to turn it into one of her own games. She gets the ball, starts back toward Brother Christopher but then stays just out of reach. She drops the ball, tempting Brother Christopher to reach for it, then picks it up and dashes a few feet away. Great fun—but not a game that will work in the long run.

Brother Christopher corrects the behavior at first using minimal direct engagement with Holly. He doesn't speak to her, give her any command, or even make eye contact; Holly might interpret any of that as part of the fun. Instead, he simply steps on the length of rope to stop her, picks it up and then brings her in close to him. After he commands her to sit, he praises her warmly. As she starts to realize she's not going to be able to set the terms of this new game, Brother Christopher begins to

introduce the "Come" command when she's at the far end of the throw. If she doesn't come right back to him, he can give her a quick leash pop with the long rope to initiate the recall. But Holly's a fast study on this one, and soon she's clearly happy playing the fetch game his way.

HOLLY TRANSFORMED

This energetic, intelligent, fun-loving dog has now learned to be well-behaved through a consistent program of exercise, fair discipline and basic obedience—not just when she wants to, but whenever her handlers demand it. When Bruce and Carolyn come to pick her up, we spend a fair amount of time being sure they know how to give the basic commands properly. After all, it isn't just Holly who needs to get used to the right kind of leash.

Remember These Things

- Play games on your terms, not the dog's.
- Don't use a retractable leash for training.
- Say a command only once.
- If a command isn't followed, give correction right away.

"Carolyn and I—and Holly—
are freer to enjoy being together."

—Bruce

Like many owners, Bruce and Carolyn need to focus on a few unfamiliar things, responding in rote ways when obedience is uppermost. Bruce has to remember not to repeat commands like "sit" several times, and not to use Holly's name when correcting. In training it is important for us to mean what we say, and not to simply repeat Holly's name machine-gun-like until she responds. Then she would be making the decision to comply. Holly should respond on the first command. Similarly, a dog's name is a positive thing, so it must be reserved for praise or for getting the dog's attention before giving a command, and not in conjunction with a correction. The latter is bad psychology.

Bruce and Carolyn are quick studies themselves, and through daily practice sessions with Holly they are soon realizing the benefits of basic obedience training. Back at home, Holly now gets regular walks in the village of Cambridge, happily staying in heel beside Carolyn even as traffic goes by. "She really likes to heel," Carolyn says, "and she loves to just walk along beside me. She has a beautiful gait, and it's really enjoyable for us both." Bruce helps her burn extra energy with vigorous outdoor games of ball-fetching. It's vigorous for Holly, but because she's so controllable, Bruce can stay in one spot.

"Carolyn and I—and Holly—are freer to enjoy being together outside in whatever environment is out there," Bruce says. "It was very restrictive to be that much on guard on her behalf." Now the guardian protecting them all is basic obedience.

As a substitute for sound obedience training, the retractable leash has been retired for good—and no one in this family misses it one bit.

Q&A:
Collars, Leashes and Other Stuff

I've heard bad things about choke and prong collars. What are they, and what's the scoop on them? Does the length of the leash matter?

There are a number of well-meaning but misguided sources of information out there preaching against the use of prong collars and slip collars on the grounds that they are cruel and invariably choke the dog no matter how they're used. The more subtle truth of the matter is that almost any collar or harness—even so-called "gentle leader" head harnesses—can cause injury if not used properly. Every owner must take the responsibility to learn how to use these training tools correctly. If that means consulting a professional for personalized help, all the better—it's well worth it.

In our opinion, prong and slip collars fitted properly on your dog's neck are both safe and far more effective than the alternatives. They allow you to make a quick, attention-getting leash pop that immediately releases, keeping the dog focused on you and on learning. Calling slip collars "choke" collars is misleading because they should never actually choke the dog.

For dogs that are at least five months old

we prefer nylon snap-around training collars. Unlike metal and nylon slip collars that go over your dog's head and are often too large, the snap-around collar goes on like a necklace and can be adjusted to fit snugly; that way you can ensure that it sits higher on your dog's neck, giving you the ability to make an appropriate correction without overcorrecting—that is, jerking too hard on the leash. To put a snap-around collar on correctly, take the clasp in your left hand and the two rings in your right hand. Facing your dog, place the collar under the neck and bring the ends up to the top of the neck, behind the ears. Clip the clasp to the movable ring. Attach your leash to the fixed ring and always heel your dog on your left side.

We find prong collars to be very good for working with larger, vigorous dogs—and entirely humane when used properly. In fact, many veterinarians and canine professionals consider the prong collar to be the safest and most effective type of training collar. Consisting of interlocking prong links that are blunt, a prong collar fits to the precise size of your dog's neck and gives an evenly distributed correction. A newer variation, called the good dog collar, is made of plastic rather than metal and looks somewhat less forbidding.

In obedience work, a six-foot leash made of leather or nylon is standard. You may also attach a rope to such a leash to create, say, a 50-foot length for working on the "come" command.

Should my dog wear his training collar all the time?

We recommend that your dog always wear a flat collar with identification and rabies tags, and a nylon training collar whenever it's safe to leave it on. The training collar allows you to get your dog under control quickly. Because there is always the remote possibility that the collar could get caught on something, such as fencing, and injure your dog, don't leave a training collar on when you can't monitor the dog. Prong collars and good dog collars are for training and leash walks only.

What kind of grooming equipment do I need for my dog?

Grooming your dog regularly not only helps you keep tabs on his overall condition and health, but also encourages bonding. As soon as you get a puppy, prepare him for routine grooming by touching and stroking him all over, especially around his paws and ears and mouth. This will prepare him for when you start clipping his nails, cleaning his ears, and brushing his teeth—grooming routines you should perform on a weekly basis. Have your breeder or another canine professional show you how to use clippers or a power grinder. Keep ear cleansing solution on hand, and when you brush your dog's teeth, be sure to use a toothbrush and toothpaste designed specifically for dogs; never use human equivalents.

All dogs require coat brushing at least

once a week and some more frequently— even every day. Depending on your dog's coat, you'll need a combination brush (slicker/bristle brush), grooming rake, pin brush, and/or shedding blade; a good flea comb is also important. Some breeds have coats that require clipping, which is best left to a professional groomer.

BOOMER

The Dog with Two Faces

Pleasant, fun-loving, affectionate, good with puppies, gentle with older dogs, the perfect companion—that's one face of Boomer. Unpredictable, wary, aggressive, untrustworthy, frightening—that's the other, disturbing face of this big, strong, beautiful dog. What accounts for his double-sided nature? And more important, can something be done to bring out the best side of Boomer, and banish the worst?

t was love at first sight for Boomer and his owner, Jacqueline, who lives in the downtown area of New York City. Jackie was out on errands one day three years ago when she passed a pet store that was sponsoring an adoption event. There were lots of dogs being offered, but Jackie was drawn to this one "really cute" puppy, a deep brownish black rottweiler mix. "His whole body was the size his head is now," Jackie remembers as she tells us about her adored Boomer, now a 115-pound solid rock of a dog. They happily played together for about an hour, but Jackie wasn't sure she was ready to bring a puppy into her life. She called back late the next day, thinking and half-hoping that someone else would have adopted him. "I remember the woman saying, 'Oh, it's you! I'm so glad. I saved him for you.' That was it."

Boomer was three months old and Jackie took him everywhere with her. He got nothing but rave reviews from acquaintances and strangers alike, and quickly grew very comfortable with all the affection. There's no question to this day that Boomer loves people.

Jackie grew up with dogs and was confident about being able to give Boomer the right start in life. "My mother had rottweilers who went to obedience school," she says, "but I figured I could do it myself." Jackie works at home, which was an advantage, and she had some success with basic obedience commands. She also took pains to socialize Boomer with other dogs. A neighbor had a rottweiler who would come over for visits, and the two dogs had a great time playing together. Even more important, Jackie took Boomer regularly to dog parks, sometimes as often as three times a day, and he would play endlessly, with no problems. He had a great disposition.

This happy relationship worked well until Boomer got to be about a year and half old. Jackie knew to expect changes, especially in a rottweiler, a breed that can become harder to handle with age. But you can see the hurt of it all—and some puzzlement—in Jackie's eyes as she tells us about the transformation in her Boomer.

It began innocently enough with a little territorial behavior, not over Jackie but over any human's affection. In a group of several people and two or three dogs, Boomer would butt in whenever someone started to pet another dog and walk around and around the circle of people making sure he was the only dog getting petted. It was actually kind of cute and funny—but then things started rising to a new level.

If Boomer was playing with another dog at the park and a third dog tried to join in, Boomer would have none of it, blocking the other dog out. Soon his reaction was more severe. "Boomer is not the kind of dog who takes a stance, growls and shows teeth," Jackie says. "To a person looking on, it seems like it's coming out of nowhere. But when another dog is approaching him, I can see in his stance and his stare that he's about to be set off. He becomes this uncontrollable dog who hits the red zone."

This can happen in the dog park or walking down the street, or even with his old rottweiler friend who used to come over but no longer does. When he senses that another dog is confronting him, if they start to stare, Boomer gets riled up—and keeps up with the escalation, reciprocating whatever the other dog's level of aggression is. "It gets to a point where he isn't hearing any commands," Jackie says.

Boomer's a big, strong fellow, and twice the fighting has left the other dog injured and requiring medical attention. Jackie now crosses the street when she sees another dog coming, and she searches out new dog parks hoping no one will recognize Boomer as the dog who "doesn't play well with others." Jackie protests, "He does play well with others—just not all dogs."

"I want him to ignore confrontations. I don't want either one of us to go through the stress anymore."

—Jackie

Boomer does indeed seem to have a Jekyll and Hyde nature. At home he sits curled at Jackie's feet when she's at her desk and sometimes gets as much of himself onto her lap as he can manage, snuggling in for rubs. And he still loves playing with other dogs—ones that don't challenge him in any way. He's especially good with puppies and very gentle with older dogs, easing up in his play, entirely sensitive to their weaknesses. He's downright submissive around female dogs, rolling over and exposing his belly—the classic canine gesture of submission.

Because of the good times, and the pleasure Boomer clearly gets from playing with his friends, Jackie keeps trying. "When he's playing and running around, you can see a smile on his face," Jackie says. "I always go back because of those good days. But if it's an uneasy day for him, I get nervous, and if there's an altercation I get embarrassed and I just want to run out of the dog park."

Boomer's Problems
- Unpredictability
- Confrontational with adult dogs
- Jealous of human attention
- Aggressive to dogs, fighting

Jackie tries to tire him out with walking before going to the park, but he still sets on any dog that for some reason upsets him. "No theory works with Boomer," she says, "none whatsoever." She is close to her wit's end and has contemplated giving him up, a notion that really disturbs her. It's obvious they have a strong bond, one that is especially meaningful to Jackie. "I got Boomer three months before my mother was diagnosed with cancer. Boomer has helped me to cope and mend, through my mother's illness, and through her loss. He's so important to me."

But Boomer can't be allowed to let his Mr. Hyde face show, and Jackie knows she has to do something. "He's made what used to be enjoyable very stressful," she says, tears in her eyes. "I want him to ignore confrontations. I don't want either one of us to go through the stress anymore. And I don't want to lose him over something so stupid as not being able to control my own dog."

What They're Thinking

BOOMER:
"My owner needs my protection."

JACKIE:
"I get nervous when we see another dog on the street."

THE MONKS:
"Boomer is given the chance to engage in classic dominance aggression; he's protecting the position he's taken in the world."

THE PROBLEM

Boomer's aggressive behavior is the result of the environment he lives in and the nature of the relationship he has with his owner. We have remarked before about the inappropriateness of treating dogs as if they're human, but it's sometimes helpful to use a human analogy to understand true canine behavior better. In that light, we see Boomer as the street kid who grew up in the city, went to a strict grade school and learned his lessons well, but when he's back out on the streets, his ingrained toughness takes over. He doesn't back down when he's challenged. "You're in my face," he says, "and I'm not putting up with it." He'll take on anyone, and he'll go to the mat.

Some dogs fight because they're afraid. Boomer fights because he feels his dominance is being challenged. When he meets a puppy or a dog friend who acknowledges his superior position, it's all fun and games. But he has no scruples about asserting himself when another dog confronts him. And he has the muscle to back it up—with consequences that are almost always unacceptable.

There's something very endearing about this big fellow, despite his problems. He's clearly capable of a lot of affection, he's extremely comfortable with human beings and he's completely trustworthy around them. The way he and Jackie are together tells us what a close relationship they have—but in the nature of that bond we also see the roots of some of his difficulties. In the city, where unpredictable situations wait around practically every corner, Boomer has learned to be on guard. He acts like he feels he has to look out for Jackie, and no doubt picks up on her anxiety, which compounds the problem. When he rises to a challenge, he's protecting her from threats as much as he is defending his rank, and her increasing anxiety about how he will react to other dogs only feeds his own wariness and readiness to fight.

Some people brand certain breeds as naturally aggressive, hostile and difficult. It's an unfair prejudice to impose on individual dogs. The issue is that some owners let big, strong dogs express socially inappropriate behavior that is exacerbated by the dogs' physical capabilities. They fail to control aggressive moves that could easily cause harm, not only to another dog, but also to an unwise human who might try to intervene at the wrong moment.

The inherent problem is not the dog's breed but the fact that he is being allowed to get away with the expression of dominant behavior that his breed can put to particularly lethal effect. We've seen canine dominance cause other types of behavioral problems in other types of dogs, including simple failure to obey the basic obedience commands. In Boomer's type of dog, his physical attributes make for more worrisome consequences.

It is true, then, that owners of certain breeds have to be especially serious about training their dogs because their bad behavior could be dangerous. But the underlying problem is the dominant behavior, not the breed.

AT THE MONASTERY

Jackie is anxious for Boomer to get the training he needs and eager to learn what she can do to be a better issuer of commands. "Boomer knows what the commands are, he knows what they mean," she tells us. "It's just a matter of whether he chooses to pay attention to them or not."

On the day he comes to us at New Skete, Boomer seems to be choosing to pay attention, and there's an air of pride to the both of them as Jackie walks Boomer through several of the basic commands. He heels reasonably well, sits on command, and stands quietly by Jackie's side while she talks with Brother Christopher.

Jackie's pride almost immediately gives way to uncertainty as she describes again her failure to elicit these good behaviors when she

"He becomes this uncontrollable dog who hits the red zone."

—Jackie

needs to. "I haven't done that great of a job, I'm finding out," she says, and it's clear that she's lost almost all confidence in her own abilities.

This is something critical to the success of the training. Dogs are able to read our posture, tone of voice and the manner in which we project ourselves. If they sense a lack of confidence, a lack of authority, they will exploit that by assuming leadership themselves. In training, the aphorism "lead or be led" is a truth that can sometimes be difficult for owners used to democratic ideals to accept. Dogs are pack animals who are very sensitive to social hierarchies, and the life of the pack unfolds much more smoothly when leadership is clearly defined, typically through the example of the alpha male or female. But effective leadership does not have to be heavy-handed and menacing. It needs to be clear, consistent and benevolent: used in the best interests of the dog and the relationship. It cannot afford to be sentimental or romantic.

As we discuss the issues with her further, she sees her own main shortcoming as not taking things "to the full level, the battle of wills between us." Her own depth of knowledge about dogs comes through in this; she has rightly sensed that dominance is the problem at hand. We talk about the possibility that Boomer has gotten the unintended message from her that it is his role to protect and to dominate. But we also want to focus her thinking away from a battle of wills—a struggle between equals—and concentrate it more on the clear, unambiguous expression of leadership.

THE MONKS' WAY

Making the Grade

Although we only raise one breed of dog here at New Skete—German shepherds—we are well aware that within that breed every individual is unique. So, from the moment of their birth through all their stages of development, we keep track of their characteristics. That means not just their physical attributes, such as whether they're on the smaller or larger end of the breed scale or what their state of health is, but also their temperament. We test them and score them, usually on a scale of 1 to 5, for such sociability issues as interactions with people, level of curiosity, and reactions to unfamiliar stimuli. The ultimate reason for this is to enable us to match each puppy with a home for which it is well suited.

To that end, we evaluate potential owners as well. We send them questionnaires, asking what their lifestyle is like and what they are looking for in a dog. How many people live in the house? How much time do they have for exercise? How chaotic or quiet are their days? The goal is a fulfilling relationship between canine and human—a happy marriage across the species.

We recall a brief moment from seeing Boomer and Jackie together at home. Boomer is lying beside Jackie on a day bed, just about a foot away, when she asks him to move in closer beside her. She says "Come" three or four times to Boomer in a small voice, bending down slightly to him with a small encouraging pat of her hand against the bedspread. She's not asking for anything major—just an inching forward—and it seems only natural for her to issue a "small" command. But there are two things amiss here. She is not giving a clear, confident command in an appropriately encouraging voice, and she's asking for something that isn't all that easy or natural for him to do, slither his hulking frame a few inches. It's never good when a command is repeated and isn't—or can't be—obeyed. Dogs need to learn to respond to a command the first time it is given. If they fail to respond, the owner needs to go to the trouble of enforcing the command and making sure the dog complies.

This may be a small matter, but it would have been better for her to reset the situation, and to give Boomer an unambiguous, confidently expressed order that he could have easily followed. We're not saying there's any major unraveling in this one small incident alone, but it does indicate to us that something about the nature of their "working" relationship needs work. Similarly, given Boomer's dominance, allowing him up on the bed or couch as Jackie does is another aspect of the way they interact that compromises her authority. It puts him on an equal level with her. In spite of the fact that Boomer loves Jackie, he needs the constant awareness that she is a benevolent alpha whom he must pay constant attention to. Thus, a down-stay on the floor for a good length of time will be an important exercise for him to master.

Jackie's shattered confidence is adding to Boomer's difficulties, creating, in a sense, a vacuum that Boomer has been filling with his own dominant behavior. We hope to restore her confidence that Boomer can learn to obey at all times, and we anticipate that renewed faith in that ability will make of herself a more effective, self-assured leader.

BOOMER'S TRAINING

As Boomer's training begins, we see right away that we're not starting from scratch: Boomer has a really good foundation in the basic exercises. But he's easily distracted, and the extra-large prong collar that he comes with doesn't seem to get his attention. Knowing that Jackie has been working with him in a somewhat relaxed way, Brother Christopher begins his sessions respectfully, determining how reliable Boomer is with the basic exercises and being careful not to come on too strong. He wants to first establish a context of relationship from which to deepen the training. Interestingly, he finds that Boomer quickly grows bored. For an energetic dog like Boomer, boredom almost immediately translates into loss of focus, and loss of focus is the kiss of death in trying to communicate leadership to a dominant dog.

Loss of focus is the kiss of death in trying to communicate leadership to a dominant dog.

So one of the first things we work on is keeping Boomer engaged. Brother Christopher picks up the pace of their training sessions, walking Boomer crisply at heel and with an authoritative manner. "Pace is so important in reflecting confidence," Brother Christopher notes. "A quick pace and quick turns broadcast confidence in yourself, and it makes him much more respectful."

Brother Christopher also works extensively on maintaining good eye contact with Boomer, which helps him earn Boomer's respect, trust and focus. "The dog learns to look to the owner for guidance, affirmation, and praise," Brother Christopher notes. "All of these things can be communicated through the eyes." Indeed, many of Boomer's confrontations with other dogs have begun with a stare-down—a warning sign

Boomer learns to stay and come

Brother Christopher guides Boomer into a sit (1) and then gives the stay command, reinforcing it with a hand gesture (2).

He teaches Boomer to come to him and not veer off to the side by stepping backwards as he calls Boomer to come (3).

With Boomer in the down position, he holds him in place with a hand gesture (4) until he's ready to call him.

that all owners should watch for. If Jackie can learn to command Boomer's attention to her own eyes instead of another dog's, she will be able to avoid most confrontations before they begin.

To that end, Brother Christopher is not averse to occasionally using a treat reward to help his focus. Boomer is particularly keen for the occasional treat, and there's nothing wrong with using that enticement to concentrate his attention, so long as it is not a continuous practice and that he gradually gets weaned from it. As the training progresses and Boomer himself gains more confidence in Brother Christopher as the leader, simply pointing at his own eyes enables Brother Christopher to focus Boomer on him.

Pace, eye contact and authoritative handling: Brother Christopher uses all these elements to keep Boomer focused on himself, engaged in the training process and, ultimately, under control no matter what.

> This is the single most magical part of our training method. We cultivate an air of certainty that does indeed work magic on dogs.

But what about that "no matter what"? Will Boomer stay in line when another dog throws down the gauntlet? We are at a bit of a disadvantage in our peaceful climes replicating the hubbub of the big city. But there is one place where we can begin to test Boomer's reaction to distraction—in the sometimes noisy confines of our own kennels.

The goal, initially, is to recreate the type of stresses Boomer experiences at home and deliberately elicit his aggressive response. So Brother Christopher takes him to the passageway through the kennels and walks him past the other dogs, who predictably start barking as he goes by. Boomer responds; the barking sets him off and he lunges toward the nearest pen. Brother Christopher immediately gives a short, sharp correction, popping the leash.

We should note here that Boomer is still wearing a prong collar, a type of training collar that has as bad—and unfair—a reputation as some breeds. Prong collars are made of metal, with a sequence of blunted prongs that briefly pinch the dog's neck and then immediately release. Many trainers and veterinarians feel they are more humane than other training collars, especially for bigger, thick-skinned dogs, because they give a correction and then release quickly, without rubbing or choking as another type of training collar might do if not used properly. They also are effective at getting the dog's attention and respect. Boomer has worn a prong collar before at home and he's familiar with it. We simply adjust a smaller size than the extra-large collar he came in with (we prefer medium to large prong collars) toward the top of his neck so that it fits snugly. It works well with him, and he gets the message to pay attention to Brother Christopher and not the dogs on the other side of the wire.

We move on to two other training techniques designed to test Boomer's obedience in the face of challenges. The first is the sidewalk routine. Brother Christopher walks Boomer along in one direction while

Remember These Things

- ☐ Work quickly and crisply when training.
- ☐ Cut off aggressive behavior with strong correction.
- ☐ Be the leader.
- ☐ Vary outings to keep the dog interested and focused on you.

his assistant, Janine, walks Holly in the other. Holly is all about playing with other dogs, and she comes through with distracting moves at Boomer. Brother Christopher corrects the least little flinch, but it's not taking much at this point. Boomer stays focused on Brother Christopher and soon pays virtually no attention to Holly's playful enticements. Then Brother Christopher puts Boomer in a static position, sitting in a stay, and lets Holly prod him with her paw. She's goading him to play, and in the past Boomer might have taken this as a challenge, especially from a dog like Holly who is fairly good-sized. Now he seems to get it and doesn't rise to the bait. By all signs, his only concern is to do what Brother Christopher says. He keeps looking up to the face above him, focused and intent.

BOOMER TRANSFORMED

In the last two weeks of his time at New Skete, Boomer gets multiple chances to fail with all of the dogs that are in for training—and he comes through with flying colors every time, showing no aggressive tendencies. One of the most rigorous tests involves putting him in a down-stay and then exposing him to Hugo's well-meaning but easily aggression-inducing offers, via physical gesture, to play. "I want to see if Boomer is going to be able to tolerate the distractedness of Hugo," Brother Christopher says. He has Boomer in a down-stay on a stretch of sidewalk as Janine brings Hugo up beside them. With only one flinch that gets a quick, standard correction, Boomer barely moves a muscle as Hugo brushes by close to him—and keeps coming back in haphazard ways that are deliberately designed to get him to respond (we have work still to do with Hugo at this point). He acts cool to it all, intermittently taking a look at Brother Christopher's face—his eyes—for confirmation.

He's also looking for confidence, and he gets it right back from Brother Christopher. This is the single most magical part of our training method. We cultivate an air of certainty that does indeed work magic on

Jackie practices down-stay with Boomer

Jackie walks Boomer at heel (1), then comes to a stop, at which point he goes into an automatic sit (2). She motions him to lie down by bringing her hand to the floor (3), then gives the stay hand gesture and strokes his back (4). Boomer is well-trained enough now that she can step over him without his breaking the down (5). She praises him warmly (6).

dogs. Boomer pays attention to the confidently delivered command, and the better we get to know this dog, the more firmly convinced we become that he is capable of unwavering obedience when given strong, unambiguous commands that keep his attention and attune his focus. It is important that he has faith in Brother Christopher's consistency. Bolstered by his handler's confident voice, he is a medal-winning Marine when it comes to obeying commands. But if he senses a weakness, he's still more than ready to step in and do what he thinks is right. He needs to feel every confidence that Jackie knows best and isn't worried. And she needs to feel every confidence that he will obey, so she won't worry. They are well and truly in this together.

Techniques like the down-stay we've taught Boomer should be a big help for Jackie in this regard. "It puts him in a controlled position that I think Jackie is going to need to take advantage of in certain situations in the city," Brother Christopher notes.

But almost more significant is just having Jackie see how well Boomer can do. When she comes to pick him up at the end of his training, Brother Christopher walks Boomer through his paces while Jackie watches unseen from inside. She is astounded at how well, and how long, he can hold the down-stay. "He's never held it that long for me," she says. "It's amazing." We can sense her confidence returning, especially when Brother Christopher has her lead Boomer through the basic obedience commands herself. He emphasizes most of all the importance of a crisp pace, so that Jackie is always the leader, always out in front and showing Boomer what's expected. And he calls her attention to how well Boomer is maintaining eye contact with her. At least for now, his focus is completely on her.

Back at home, Jackie puts her confidence in the commands she now gives with more authority. She adopts a program at home that establishes the couch and bed as off-limits, and incorporates extended down-stays of at least thirty minutes to her daily regimen. She practices with Boomer twice daily for sessions of ten to fifteen minutes apiece, and at the dog park, we have recommended that Jackie initially work Boomer around the other dogs on leash, to get a sense of his emotional barometer and to re-emphasize her leadership. We have also instructed her to make use of a soft muzzle whenever she is nervous as a preventive measure to help stop his tendency to pick fights. There have been moments when Boomer has tested her, when he has looked like he is about to rise to a challenge. Jackie is well-attuned to those moments; that's a skill she has always had. But the new skill that makes all the difference is her immediate, confident willingness to take the dominant role in their relationship. "I'm more in control," she says, "and he's easier to control, much more responsive to my commands than before." The dark side of Boomer fades more from memory with each successful outing, and the sunny side of this lovable dog shines clear.

Q&A:
Doggie Workout

We have a big fenced-in yard and the dogs are free to roam. We let them out there to do their business, and to play and romp. Do they need more exercise than this?

You bet! No matter how many dogs you have, you need to be actively involved in exercising and training them. That means daily walks off the property and one-on-one handling in cases where there are two or more dogs. While a fenced-in yard gives your dogs valuable outdoor time, it's absolutely no substitute for routine exercise with you. If you have two or more dogs, you'll most likely see them playing and running around together, but if you don't also work with them yourself, you'll end up in a situation where the dogs bond with each other but not with you. Single dogs definitely don't get enough exercise just from being out in the yard. They often just lie around or sleep, and they sometimes develop digging or excessive barking behavior to relieve their boredom.

Perhaps an attitude adjustment is in order—for you. Rather than looking at exercise as an unwelcome chore, think of the positives that it brings both you and your dog. Exercise can be fun, especially if you incorporate some obedience training into your routine. For your dog, regular walks provide mental as well as physical stimulation, particularly if you have several different routes you can follow. And don't overlook the fact that a good, vigorous walk is beneficial for your own health. We know one dog owner who wears a pedometer to track the walking he does with his dog. He sets goals, so that even when he's feeling less than inspired, there's one more motivation to grab the leash and hit the sidewalk— he's got to get his steps in for the day!

A reasonable minimum for adult dogs is two 20- to 30-minute walks a day; some sporting, retrieving and herding breeds require much more than that. A word of caution for younger dogs who are still developing: no Frisbee or hard running. Beyond that, though, get out there and walk!

How do you feel about dog parks?

Dog parks have their value but they should never be seen as a substitute for a walk. As we've said, formal walks with your dog are a necessary part of building a good relationship. If you do visit a dog park as well, be aware of the pros and cons. Time at the park can increase your dog's social skills, but it's not unknown for bullying and dog fighting to occur at dog parks and for your dog to learn bad habits from other dogs.

To use a dog park most beneficially, exercise your dog thoroughly first. Then check who's there before you let your dog loose, watching for any problematic behavior in other dogs. If your dog is young and unfamiliar with the setting, accustom her to the situation by walking her around the perimeter first. Take the leash off your dog before you go in and put it on before you come out. Finally, always keep an eye on your dog and learn to read the body language of all dogs so that you can act preventively should warning signs occur.

What kinds of games are good to play with my dog?

Fetch is a traditional game that never gets old and is of great benefit to building a strong relationship with your dog. Teach your dog to release the ball or stick by using two articles and rotating the retrieve between them. Another wonderful game is Frisbee, though it's important to be careful with a younger dog: Jumping up for a catch can strain young muscles and joints.

Use your imagination to come up with other games. On a walk in the woods you can play hide-and-seek by putting your dog in a sit-stay and then hiding up the path and calling "Come," letting your dog find you. Dogs also love scent games. Hide favorite articles in your home and have your dog try to find them. Finally, there are organized games such as flyball and agility that dogs love. You can even put obstacles in your yard for your dog to play with once he understands the nature of the game.

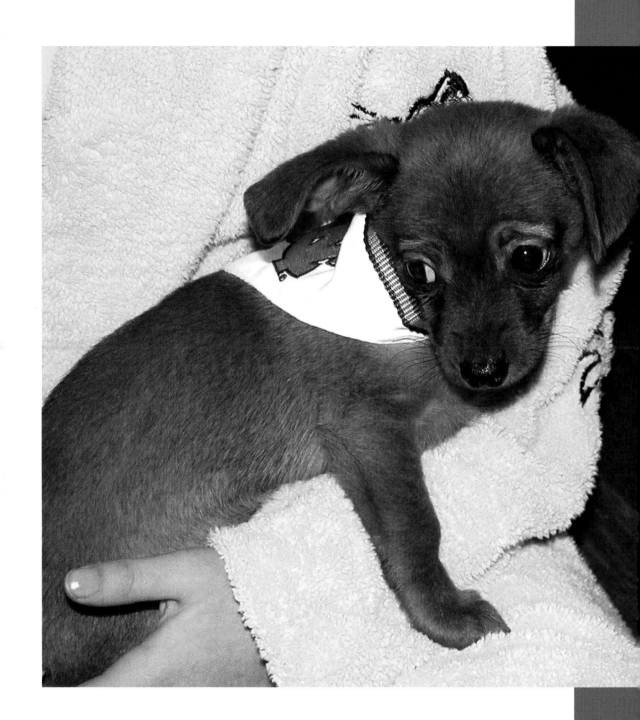

The Basics
Sit ●
Heel ○
Stay ●
Down ●
Come ○

SWEET PUPPY

What's in a Name?

Yes, it's his real name, and yes, there's a story behind it. But there's more of a story to how this cute little dog ended up causing so much trouble. In a house with three children under ten, it's not surprising the parents find no time for doggie discipline. But Sweet Puppy's annoying ways still need reining in. The good news? With some basic training, this rose by another name can once again smell sweet.

Bobby was coming home from a business trip late one night when he heard a whimpering sound coming from a small black bag sitting in the airport concourse. He went over to check, looked inside and saw a tiny brown dog. He took the bag down to baggage claim to turn the dog in, thinking someone had lost it, but they told him they couldn't accept a living creature. Bobby looked inside the bag again and saw a note. It said, "Please take care of Sweet Puppy. I can't take care of him anymore." There were a few treats scattered in the bottom of the bag.

"I had always wanted a dog," Bobby says remembering the moment, "but had been prohibited from having one. So I viewed this as Nature smiling on me." Bobby decided then and there to take "Sweet Puppy" home with him.

When he got to his car, he took Sweet Puppy, a miniature dachshund-Pomeranian mix weighing about three pounds, out of the bag and looked him over. He was clean and obviously had been well cared for. Bobby sat him in his lap for the ride home, and they bonded right away. As Bobby tells his story, Sweet Puppy lies curled in the crook of Bobby's arm, contentment writ large on his tiny features.

Susan wasn't exactly thrilled with the new addition at first. She found out about Sweet Puppy at three that morning, when a rustling noise awakened her. She screamed, thinking a wild animal had somehow gotten into the house. When Jacqueline, who is nine now, woke the next morning, she let out a different kind of scream—one of delight. Her two younger brothers, Jake and Dylan, came rushing in, and from that moment on, there was no question: This family had a new dog.

He quickly became a bona fide member of the family, going with them wherever they went. "When he was little, I treated him like we did when we had babies," Bobby says. He is indeed a very cuddly little package and it's not too hard to imagine why his previous owner gave him his name. He's also playful with the kids, which they just adore. They actually spend more time playing with him than with any of their toys or video games. Not a bad development, one would think, but sometimes things get a little out of hand. One of their favorite games is "Chase the Boys." The two boys run around, jumping up on couches and beds with Sweet Puppy in hot pursuit and squeals of excitement all around. But when he catches up to them, he often nips at their clothing or their heels—or sometimes arms and legs. The kids' reaction only seems to goad Sweet Puppy on, and the inevitable result is one or more of the children in tears, and Sweet Puppy relegated to his crate, where he himself can put up an annoying, whining cry.

As for obedience, there's little of it to be seen in this admittedly adorable creature. "Our training method has been benign neglect," says Bobby, who clearly has a special relationship with Sweet Puppy but just hasn't had the time to give him the kind of regular training that's

Sweet Puppy's Problems

- Nipping
- Whining and crying in crate
- Barking at strangers, other dogs, noises and moving objects like a sweeping broom
- Ignoring commands

necessary to cement good behavior. It's not just that they've never corrected or chastised him effectively; they haven't rewarded him for good behavior either. "We do try to yap at him when he does things wrong," Bobby goes on, "but the training has been less than rigorous."

"Our training method has been benign neglect."

—Bobby

The consequences are clear. Sweet Puppy won't sit or stay on command, cries and whines when he's left alone in his crate, yaps at strangers, barks at other dogs incessantly, has house-training issues, is destructive when left alone outside the crate and even attacks the broom when Susan tries to sweep the floor in the kitchen. Of course worst of all, Sweet Puppy isn't shy about using his teeth with the children. "They tell him no," Bobby says, "and he doesn't listen." Because the kids need comforting at that point, it's hard for Bobby to take time to correct Sweet Puppy beyond getting him out of the way in his crate. And fifteen minutes later, the children are ready for more, encouraging Sweet Puppy to a new round of play that leads to more nipping, so there's little reason for Sweet Puppy to think anything's unacceptable about it.

The family wants to be able to control their little dog better, but the parents can't imagine finding the time they know they need to devote to his training. Bobby heads the liver program at a major, prestigious hospital in New York City, so he's often home late or away at conferences. Susan has to manage getting three children under the age of ten to school and other activities and keeping the household running. "Because of the time constraints on both of us," Susan says, "we need instruction on what's the most efficient way to train Sweet Puppy."

THE PROBLEM

Sweet Puppy is almost too sweet for his own good. His affectionate nature and winning ways—on top of the fact that neither Bobby nor Susan has time for training—have led to him becoming a rather spoiled dog who can get away with an awful lot. The worst of his misbehaviors don't seem all that bad, coming from so small a package; that's partly why he gets away with so much. Actually, this is quite common with small dogs, whose owners tend to put up with a lot more than owners with big dogs. Because these dogs are so small, owners try to manage things without the formal discipline of obedience training, which requires time and commitment that many owners will avoid if at all possible. But even a small dog like Sweet Puppy can really hurt someone with nipping that gets out of control. And misbehavior should never be tolerated anyway. For one thing, it's keeping the relationship between this dog and his human family from being as enjoyable and enriching as it could be. Why settle for frustration?

Dominance issues of the kind we've seen with other *Divine Canine* dogs may very well be at play here, to a limited extent and with one significant wrinkle. Bobby and Susan have both talked about Sweet Puppy being beta to Bobby's alpha: submissive to Bobby, but disobedient and dominant with everyone—and everything—else. "This dog thinks he's huge, at least on the inside," Bobby says explaining Sweet Puppy's tendency to bark at all manner of other dogs, including those who are physically much bigger: Dobermans, German shepherds and Labrador retrievers.

Susan tells a story that illustrates how dominant Sweet Puppy has at times been over her. Shortly after the dog joined the family, Bobby was away at a conference, and at night Sweet Puppy would try to get up on her bed. When Susan would try to pick him up to shift him a little, Sweet Puppy turned sour, growling and even nipping at her. Determined to hold on to some authority, Susan protectively wrapped her hands up in her bathrobe and picked a protesting Sweet Puppy up. "After about a week of this," Susan remembers, "he stopped the growling and was submissive enough that I could pick him up without him demonstrating to me, 'Hello, you have no business touching me.'" Nevertheless, Sweet Puppy was still sleeping on the beds, still up on the couch, still being allowed to stay on the same level as his human counterparts.

Beyond dominance issues, though, what's going on here becomes clearer when you pay attention to the ways Bobby talks about Sweet Puppy. He was treated "like a baby," loved like one of the kids, taken everywhere with them, showered with affection, and so on. In other words, he is regarded as an intimate member of their *human* family.

Sweet Puppy himself undoubtedly sees things in different terms. To him, he's part of a *canine* pack, and while he defers to Alpha Bobby, he still likes to have fun with the rest of the pack as he naturally would with other dogs. While there may have been an element of dominance expression in Sweet Puppy's first instances of nipping and growling at Susan, nipping at the kids' heels is classic play behavior, precisely as one would see it in the wolf pack, where members interact with each other principally by way of their mouths. Sweet Puppy is just having a good time being a puppy in the pack. At best guess he's still only about a year old, and to him the children are just other puppies, his canine siblings.

His nipping during these play sessions is benign enough that the kids constantly come back for more. But his dog-based version of play isn't acceptable in a house where other people's children are often around, and where it represents the fact that Sweet Puppy can get away with just about anything. It's part of an overall picture where canine rules apply more than human ones.

At the same time, there's a sense in which the problem involves canine rules not applying as fully as they would in a real pack. When puppies frolic and nip, the nips are returned; part of this is the bigger pups and older dogs asserting their position, but it's also a kind of self-enforced discipline among equals that defines the limits of tolerable

SWEET PUPPY:
"A little nip—it's all part of the fun!"

THE CHILDREN:
"He's so much fun—except
when he nips!"

THE MONKS:
"Sweet Puppy is acting naturally,
like a wolf pup in a pack but with
no disciplinary constraint."

behavior and that establishes a clear pecking order. Lo and behold for Sweet Puppy, nobody nips back, and he takes this to mean that anything goes.

The core of the problem, then, is that Sweet Puppy lives in a human environment where proper canine behavior hasn't been properly taught, and where the little that has isn't being enforced. For all the love he receives, Sweet Puppy lacks the leadership he so desperately needs. He gets to do what he wants, but neither he nor his human family is getting to realize the benefits of a good, healthy human-canine relationship.

AT THE MONASTERY

The family has mixed emotions about leaving Sweet Puppy with us for four weeks. Susan is focused not only on getting Sweet Puppy the training he needs but also on getting a break for herself, even if temporary. "Part of me is very excited about having one less person to think about," she says. But she's also aware how sad the children will be; it will feel like a much longer time to them, as if Sweet Puppy is gone forever. And she admits that this little fellow has gotten under her skin, too—she means this in the good way here. Bobby is not in the least bit eager to be without his little companion. "You love your dog the way you love your kids," he says, acknowledging how much he'll miss their quiet times together during early-morning or late-night walks through a peaceful neighborhood, or just those moments of lap-time when the unfettered affection flows both ways.

"This dog thinks he's huge, at least on the inside."

—Bobby

We've been impressed from the start with the bond between this man and this dog. Bobby is an extremely busy doctor with myriad professional responsibilities. He touches many people's lives and has to deal on a daily basis with stressful situations that sometimes involve life or death decisions. It can all be somewhat dehumanizing, but when Bobby talks about the moments he gets with Sweet Puppy, his eyes shine with how important his connection is to this little dog he rescued, the little dog he "always wanted." These times represent important cornerstones in his life.

So we completely understand that when Bobby comes home from a stressful day, the last thing he wants to do is anything assertive or anything that might, in his thinking, jeopardize that bond. Sweet Puppy often chews on Bobby's fingers during laptime or otherwise acts up, and it's clear Bobby would rather just chill out and let things be than try to enforce discipline on this little dog who always is so overjoyed to see him—and brings him nothing more problematic than a little whining and barking and, well, nipping and chewing every now and then. In many ways, for Bobby the status quo is working just fine.

What we'd like to invite him to realize—and what we discuss on the phone as the family prepares to leave Sweet Puppy with us—is that Bobby can actually get into a relationship with Sweet Puppy that is much more fulfilling and much more enjoyable for both of them if he does take the time to follow through on obedience, and adds more structure to Sweet Puppy's life. This little dog clearly needs that, and we sense that Bobby is ready to indeed follow through—once someone else does the "hands-on work" of building a foundation of basic obedience. He needs a helping hand—again, completely understandable—and we're ready to provide it.

It is not without thought that at this stage we focus on Bobby's interactions with Sweet Puppy rather than any other member of the family. He has expressed that he feels responsible for Sweet Puppy being in the family in the first place and thus wants to take on the responsibility for his training. But beyond that, Bobby is clearly the one member of the family who has an "in" with Sweet Puppy that will enable him to more easily reinforce and cement the lessons Sweet Puppy learns with us. However, given the fact that she will be the one home during the day, Susan will need to be an active part of the picture once Sweet Puppy returns after the training. We fully expect that once Bobby follows through and communicates to Sweet Puppy through his actions that some new rules now apply and then works with Susan, Susan will have little trouble exerting her own authority as well.

As for the children, who are now nine, seven and three, they're too young to be asked to discipline their favorite playmate. We stress that Bobby and Susan will have to be forthright about controlling those playtimes and keeping the kids from being too rambunctious with Sweet

Puppy. They need to be the leaders and not expect too much from their children in this regard.

Finally, we call attention once again to the importance of treating Sweet Puppy as a dog, not as a person. Sweet Puppy is not "one less person to think about," as Susan has said, and shouldn't really be loved "as you love your children," in Bobby's words. A dog has its own dignity as a dog. Everyone in the family will be better off, and happier, when the dog plays the role of dog, and the people take on their appropriate leadership roles.

SWEET PUPPY'S TRAINING

We know from Sweet Puppy's history that he has had no formal training, no foundation in the basic obedience commands. In fact, Bobby has told us that Sweet Puppy has never even worn any kind of collar, let alone a training collar; Bobby has always used a harness for walks. So Brother Christopher works very gently with Sweet Puppy, using a flat nylon collar at first rather than a training collar. Sweet Puppy has grown since Bobby first found him but still weighs only six pounds, so Brother Christopher will carefully calibrate his corrective gestures with the leash and handle him with a very light touch.

Sweet Puppy takes surprisingly well to the collar and he's very eager as Brother Christopher takes him out on the grass for his first training session. He tends to bounce and prance along at the end of the leash, clearly not exactly sure what's going on, and a little nervous. But the tail is wagging—always a good sign.

For one of the first attempts at a sit, Brother Christopher gets right down beside Sweet Puppy, who follows his upward hand gesture and sits down, with a little helpful guidance from Brother Christopher's hand placed on his back near the tail. When Sweet Puppy tries to roll over submissively, Brother Christopher keeps him upright by holding his head in his hand and then, holding the leash very near the collar, repositioning Sweet Puppy into a proper sit. Sweet Puppy looks up for reassurance, and Brother Christopher praises him by repeating "Yes" several times in a soft, soothing voice. He also pets his chest with smooth, upward strokes. Because they are starting from scratch, his first sessions with Sweet Puppy are preliminary: giving Sweet Puppy a context in which to adjust to his leadership.

At this early stage, Brother Christopher doesn't enforce a strict heel; in fact, he never uses the word, only saying "Let's go!" to get Sweet Puppy up and following him again. Everything is taken very slowly and gently. And because Sweet Puppy is so inherently exuberant, Brother Christopher keeps his praise just a little muted, to avoiding ramping him up.

The progress even in this first session is quite impressive. "What a smart little guy," Brother Christopher says to Sweet Puppy as they keep walking around, moving into a sit every so often.

As the lessons continue, Brother Christopher eventually switches to a training collar that will give just a little more correction when Sweet Puppy strays away from Brother Christopher's side or doesn't hold a sit. Brother Christopher uses a quick but relatively quiet "Eh!" as a verbal correction, and sometimes a similarly voiced "No." Patience is key at this early stage, and Brother Christopher works diligently to keep the sessions positive and encouraging. To encourage eye contact, he makes a kissing, smooching noise that makes Sweet Puppy look up to his face, at which point Brother Christopher is pointing to his own eyes, saying, "Watch me, Good Boy!"

With heel and sit coming along nicely, soon they're working on stay. At first Brother Christopher barely moves away from Sweet Puppy, keeping the leash a bit high and taut and giving the verbal command and the open-palm hand gesture in front of Sweet Puppy's face. He does this initially to accustom Sweet Puppy to someone walking around and behind him without allowing him to break the stay. Often dogs can be uncomfortable with movement behind them and the taut leash helps keep

Sweet Puppy learns sit-stay

Brother Christopher has Sweet Puppy sit, then keeps most of the leash folded up in his hand, holding it near the collar so he can give a mild correction if necessary (1). He tells Sweet Puppy to stay, then helps him hold the position with slight upward tension on the leash (2). Sweet Puppy stays sitting, looking up at Brother Christopher, and doesn't break even when Brother Christopher bounces up (3).

Sweet Puppy learns down-stay

Brother Christopher tells Sweet Puppy to sit and stay by bring his hand in front of Sweet Puppy's face (1). He tells him "Down" and brings his hand down to the ground, encouraging him into the position with the gesture and by bringing the leash down in his other hand (2). He tells Sweet Puppy to stay in the down position with the same open-palm gesture used for sit-stay (3).

No Dull Boys Here

"All work and no play make Jack a dull boy." It's an old aphorism, but it's one we hew to at New Skete. Training, you might say, is the "work" part of what we do with dogs. There's a whole other aspect to building a good relationship that's just as important.

One of the first things we tell people who will be taking one of our puppies is how important it is to exercise them sufficiently and properly. New Skete puppies get exercise almost from the day they are born. We use a simple rolled-up wad of paper towel to mimic a ball and toss it across the kennel floor so puppies can learn about fetching a real ball while they're still too small to play with one. We exercise them out on the grass, using a rapid series of encouraging hand claps to urge them to romp along with us. We walk them up short flights of outdoor stone steps—shallow enough for their still-tiny frames to handle. And we encourage sessions of command-free play on a routine basis.

We recommend that you give your dog two vigorous walks a day that include a play session of fetch or something else your dog enjoys. This will give your dog the kind of energy-releasing stimulation that will actually enable him to be included more naturally in your life. The play is just as important as the work.

them in place until they become familiar with this. Corrections involve a very slight little pop straight up on the leash that puts the dog right in the spot where he was told to stay, and the position is held for several seconds. Getting ready to move forward, Brother Christopher now uses the heel command, and he keeps Sweet Puppy from bouncing and prancing with gentle leash corrections that keep him focused and alert. Soon those little front legs are trotting along but tending to come up off the ground less and less.

They also begin to work on down. Down starts from the sit position. Initially, Brother Christopher simply lifts Sweet Puppy's front paws and moves him into a down position as he says the command. He keeps his left hand gently on the dog's back to keep him in place. Once Sweet Puppy has a clear sense of the command, Brother Christopher goes to the next stage. With Sweet Puppy in a sit and Brother Christopher standing at a ninety-degree angle facing him, he makes a gentle sweeping-down motion with his right hand in front of Sweet Puppy's face and gently leads Sweet Puppy down to the ground as he gives the command. Once his body is prone, Sweet Puppy starts to roll over. "I keep that down very, very brief at this stage," Brother Christopher says, "and I'm not concerned if he rolls over. I'm more concerned with his willingness to go into a down position at first. Once that occurs, I'll make sure he doesn't roll over." This happens more quickly than expected. As he repositions Sweet Puppy from rolling over on his side, soon the smart little dog is holding the position with a simple "Stay" command.

Remember These Things

- [ ] With a very small dog, keep corrections very slight.
- [ ] Before tackling problems, build a foundation of obedience.
- [ ] Give commands to replace problematic reactions with good behavior.

Sweet Puppy's Progress

After two weeks of work, Sweet Puppy is doing very well with all five obedience commands, especially the sit, stay and down commands that Brother Christopher has been emphasizing. But how do these relate to solving Sweet Puppy's nipping and barking problems?

"The first way of approaching a solution to these problems," Brother Christopher explains, "is through the dog's knowledge and understanding of the basic obedience exercises." Whenever we want to stop some undesired behavior, we always have to replace it with one that is desired and that the dog understands. With this foundation of the five basic exercises now in place, we can set up situations that draw out Sweet Puppy's inclination to bark or nip but then replace it with good behavior that he already understands.

"Sweet Puppy can be yippy. But with a quick little correction with the leash, you can easily turn him off."
—Brother Christopher

We have one ready-made form of distraction in our own kennel, where frequently a chorus of barking serves as a backdrop. As Sweet Puppy has become more comfortable with this new environment, he has tended to start barking himself in response during his own training sessions. It's just what Brother Christopher wants, because it allows him to do two things to help address the problem. First, he can give a quick leash correction with a short "No!" when Sweet Puppy starts to bark; and it does indeed turn him off. And Brother Christopher can also refocus Sweet Puppy's attention to any of the obedience commands he's now quite proficient at. His barking is at times reactive (triggered by other dogs getting attention or by their own barking) and at times territorial (a stranger invading his space), so immediately going into an obedience drill not only shifts his attention from defending his "turf," but it also gives him reassurance. His human leader is telling him that everything is all right, and that it's time for him to do what he now does best: obey commands.

SWEET PUPPY TRANSFORMED

As the training shifts into the final weeks of the program, Brother Christopher proofs Sweet Puppy's obedience by working him in close proximity to other dogs. Such distractions provoke occasional mistakes that give Brother Christopher the opportunity to make helpful corrections that reinforce Sweet Puppy's understanding of the exercises and make them more easily applicable to everyday situations. The most amusing of these sessions features Sweet Puppy working flawlessly alongside Boomer, the 115-pound rottweiler mix!

We have one more test for Sweet Puppy. Calling on the services of some local children, we put Sweet Puppy in a situation where, in the past, he might have started nipping at heels. We have the children romp and play around while Brother Christopher puts Sweet Puppy in a down-stay. He's so good at this now that with very little correction he holds the position and doesn't fall prey to the temptation, even though he's clearly interested in the children. He seems confident about his own abilities, more comfortable, and is definitely more controllable. More impressively, after the children finish with their play session, they come over and greet Sweet Puppy warmly, and his response is nice and controlled. He loves the interaction, but he's not out of control: He's well-behaved and affectionate.

Bobby comes to pick Sweet Puppy up at the end of the four weeks and spends several hours absorbing the training. He's truly astounded at how well-behaved Sweet Puppy is and listens carefully as Brother Christopher instructs him in handling Sweet Puppy on the leash and

An exciting world of possibility awaits in the family's relationship with Sweet Puppy.

how to give commands and make corrections—being firm but not too strong and by all means resisting the urge to let Sweet Puppy get away with misbehaviors.

We recommend that for the next week or two Sweet Puppy be kept on a leash in the house. It can hang loose, but it's a vital way to give a quick physical correction when a problem behavior emerges. Soon the verbal correction will be sufficient, but we also point out that the most important thing is to replace the bad behavior with something positive—obeying a command—and that he and Susan be consistent with this. That's how the foundation of training will come to the rescue. When a visitor comes into the house, for example, instead of letting Sweet Puppy bark, Bobby will bring Sweet Puppy up to the visitor on leash, then get him to sit and stay in front of the person so that a more formal, controlled "introduction" can take place. This will be a far cry from the way it used to be when Sweet Puppy would freely and wildly bark and jump up on the visitor.

The children will of course still want to play with Sweet Puppy, and they should, but we want the parents to stay in control of the situation and not let things get out of hand. As they get older, the children will enjoy new, more positive ways of interacting with Sweet Puppy—taking him for walks that don't break down into chaotic affairs, reinforcing the basic commands, even teaching him all sorts of new tricks. An exciting world of possibilities awaits in their relationship with Sweet Puppy.

Everything we discuss with Bobby is aimed at encouraging him and the family to respect and honor Sweet Puppy's true nature as a dog. One thing we prescribe is that they carry him around less (if at all!), treating him less "like a baby" and more like a dog. We know that Bobby thrives on the love he gets from Sweet Puppy and that he lavishes in return, so we reassure him that following through on obedience will actually deepen their connectedness. We suggest that when Bobby wants to be really affectionate with Sweet Puppy that he get down on the floor and interact with him, rather than letting Sweet Puppy come up on the chair or bed. Sweet Puppy will be more relaxed and happier knowing and following the rules, and that can only strengthen the bond between humans and canine.

This sweet little dog that was found in a small black bag at the airport will always be a puppy by name, but we hope that, with a foundation of training in place, both he and his family can realize all the marvelous potential of a more mature relationship. Sweet Puppy deserves nothing less.

Q&A: Training Basics

Can I do obedience training myself, or should I use a professional? Are private lessons better than group ones?

You can certainly do obedience training on your own, but you have to be willing to commit to the process—willing to educate yourself thoroughly on the proper techniques and also willing and able to dedicate the time it takes. Even if you can seriously commit to being your dog's trainer, there are real advantages to getting professional help. Qualified professionals offer a wealth of experience and a broad perspective. They can put you and your dog on the right track from the start, and they can course-correct your own training regimen—we often can't see the mistakes we're making.

For starting out, we prefer private, in-house training to group classes. Private sessions give you and your dog the chance to learn in calm, nondistracting circumstances under the watchful eye of the trainer; it's also the best place to address issues that naturally arise in the home setting. Residency training such as what we offer here at New Skete is another good alternative, but be sure it includes a thorough seminar and demonstration for you—that you get training too! Having a professional establish the basics doesn't let you off the hook. You and everyone in your family always have to be involved in practicing and applying the training afterwards. Once basic training is in place, group classes can be a valuable follow-up, helping to socialize your dog with other dogs and people, and proofing your dog's training in the face of distractions.

How do I decide among all the trainers listed in the telephone directory?

Rather than picking names from the telephone book, get recommendations from your veterinarian, your groomer, or dog-owning friends. Another valuable resource is the Internet, which can give you much more information than a mere directory listing or "yellow pages" advertisement. The International Association of Canine Professionals, www.dogpro.org, and the National Association of Dog Obedience Instructors, www.nadoi.org, are two outstanding organizations dedicated to excellence in the training field; they both have extensive databases of member trainers, and you'll undoubtedly be able to find one near you.

When you contact prospective trainers, interview them about their approach. Remember that some trainers will be generalists, while others may have particular areas they specialize in. Ask if it's possible to visit their establishment and observe them working with a dog; experienced trainers won't have a problem with this. Above all, look for professionalism, experience—and a genuine love for dogs.

Some trainers advertise "purely positive training." Is that a good thing?

That phrase indicates the trainer employs food rewards and verbal praise (or reinforcement with a tool called a "clicker") exclusively to shape behavior, with no leash correction or disciplinary action of any kind. While positive reinforcement—the association of praise and reward with good behavior—is important in all forms of dog training, we believe purely positive training can have significant limitations. We're also bothered by the moralizing tone of its practitioners, which suggests that other approaches are inhumane and mean-spirited. Purely positive trainers have no corner on the market of compassion and commitment to the welfare of dogs. Our experience unequivocally shows that dogs can be trained humanely and effectively—more effectively, in our opinion—with a balanced approach of praise and appropriate correction. Further, when misbehavior borders on being dangerous—if, for example, your dog lunges at cars—punishment administered firmly but without anger is not only legitimate but in your dog's best interests.

How your dog responds ultimately determines whether a given training method has succeeded or failed. Is good behavior sticking? Is your dog's personality blossoming? If it is, all well and good. But if problems persist, or new ones arise, we only advise that you not limit the legitimate tools and techniques available to help you train your dog.

My dog knows the basics. Now I want to try teaching her some "fancy stuff," like flyball or agility work. How do I take my dog to the next level?

For more advanced forms of training, it's usually best to work with a club. Do an Internet search to learn about options in your area. Books and videos can give you information on what's appropriate for your dog. But remember: The point of working on this with your dog is not to teach her "fancy stuff" but to enrich your relationship and help it reach its potential.

HARLEY

A Mouthful of Dominant Dog

This golden boy is a treasure to his family but also a drain on their resources of patience. Harley's only one but still has all the boisterousness of a much younger pup. He jumps, he barks, he dashes about and throws himself at people. But worst of all, he "mouths," grabbing at furniture, clothing, arms and legs—anything that gets a reaction. It's all part of his game—and the game never ends with Harley. Can we find this dog's "off" button, and teach his family how to use it?

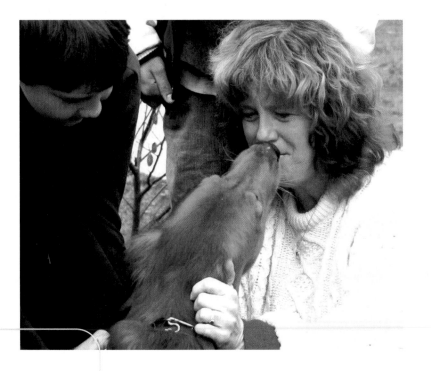

Harley is the classic American dog, living the suburban life in New Jersey with Mary Ellen and her two sons, Chris, sixteen, and Rob, thirteen. He's purebred golden retriever, and came to the family in the classic way. They had always had dogs, but when their last one, a retriever-Labrador mix, died at thirteen, they'd stayed without one for a year. The boys had started begging, and Mary Ellen secretly wanted another dog as well, so one weekend when both boys were away, she made her move. When the boys returned, sitting in the middle of Rob's bed—replacing his normal array of stuffed animals, mostly dogs—was Harley, an eight-week-old puppy. The two of them in particular bonded instantly, but Harley was a happy part of the whole family right away.

He even seemed relatively calm at first, but according to Mary Ellen, that didn't last long. "All puppies chew on things. That seemed normal and appropriate. But after a couple of months, I realized it was a problem." Harley was grabbing at her shoes, and nipping at the backs of her pants legs as she walked. He was getting more and more boisterous with the boys and their friends, and Mary Ellen was particularly concerned about him jumping up on people, since he was getting bigger and more capable of knocking someone down.

"I love his personality, but I just want him to be calm."

—Chris

But that's really only the tip of the iceberg. Harley digs in the garden—big, expanding pits that he'll keep going at if no one stops him. He grabs at the still-attached branches of thick-limbed bushes. Inside he playfully tries to attack Mary Ellen's hair dryer in the morning, he goes for the mop or the broom, he won't let Chris play the guitar without trying to jump up on him—and he can't be left alone in the house, because he destroys furniture, tearing into upholstery and cushions and whatever he can get his muzzle around.

Speaking of muzzles, the family has finally resorted to an actual muzzle when there are lots of people around. "We're a really close family," says Mary Ellen, "and we're together as much as possible. We live near the high school and the middle school, and we have an open house policy for kids to come in and out." So there's always lots of commotion—and lots of opportunity for Harley to get out of control. And physical muzzling—much as they all seem to hate it—has been the only thing that's worked.

We listen as some of Chris's and Rob's friends and the two boys sit around talking about Harley, even while Harley is there at their feet—and sometimes up on the couch with them—showing off some of his best misbehaviors. He grabs onto a sneaker—foot inside!—and starts up a tug of war. He bites on his leash—and on a cushion. He mouths at people's wrists and licks at their hands, and paws at them from a rolled-over position, the center of attention there in the middle of the floor.

Rob worries that some of his friends don't come over as often because they don't like Harley's ways and are actually afraid of him. The ones who are there, though, profess to coming over just as much as always. "It's fun being here because you never know what's going to happen next with him," says one of them as he interacts with Harley, playfully slapping lightly around his mouth and getting Harley to respond with mouthing. "But after twenty minutes of getting your arm chewed on, it's not fun anymore." Responding to the general consensus, Chris puts the soft cloth muzzle over Harley's mouth.

Instantly he's a different dog, lying down quietly on the floor, not responding or trying to interact with anyone. He does get up and go over to one of the friends after a couple of minutes. "He's asking you to take it off," says Chris. And after a few more minutes—they usually wait about fifteen—they do take the muzzle off. Harley remains quieter for a while, and when he starts to act up, Rob shows him the muzzle. Harley's big worried golden retriever eyebrows say it all. But truth to tell, Rob feels just as upset about this way of handling Harley. As Chris puts it, "It's sad to see him like this. He looks depressed."

They all know it's a stopgap solution they don't really find acceptable. What they tend to do more often is sequester Harley when people are over. Mary Ellen in particular feels bad about this. "I'm a believer that the dog should just be part of the family. Right now I can't follow that 100 percent because of his behavior." When the doorbell rings now, an air of tension spreads through the house. Will someone put Harley away? Will he get to "play" with the visitors for a while, and if so, who's going to watch him and make sure he doesn't get too far out of control? Is somebody holding him so he doesn't flatten people when they come

Harley's Problems
- Jumping up
- Mouthing
- Not obeying commands
- Always interrupting activities

in the door? Harley usually gets put away somewhere, "but it's unrealistic," says Mary Ellen. "He has to be integrated into the family."

The boys want things to work better as well. "I love his personality," says Chris, "but I just want him to be calm." Rob, who everyone acknowledges is closest to Harley, is concerned that his mom is thinking about needing to get rid of Harley. "I just want his jumpiness and craziness to go away," he says, the love and worry big in his eyes.

Having heard of us and visited us here at the New Skete monastery, Mary Ellen made inquiries and managed to get Harley into our training program. She is full of hope—something

HARLEY:
"Come on! Play tug with me! That's it!"

FRIEND:
"I really don't appreciate
being a chew toy."

THE MONKS:
"Harley has found
an effective way
to gain attention.
He craves it."

"After twenty minutes of getting your
arm chewed on, it's not fun anymore."

—A friend of Rob and Chris

we always like to see. And we encourage her to talk about it. "My hope for Harley—because he's such an intelligent, loving dog—is that some of his behaviors will get under control so I won't have to worry about the safety of people, that he'll just listen, and that we can integrate him into everything that we do."

There are regrets on her part as well. "I do feel I failed him," Mary Ellen says. "Part of love is discipline, and I do feel I've failed at the discipline." But she sees a chance to get a fresh start, and that's always a good place to begin. "This opportunity is like a gift. I know it's not a simple cure-all. But I have a really positive feeling it's going to make a big difference in his life, and in our lives."

THE PROBLEM

We're seeing in Harley what we've seen in so many other dogs, including quite a few in *Divine Canine*. Harley's problem is dominance—taking an inappropriate position of authority and leadership in his family's pack.

Harley's form of dominance differs from several of those we've seen. There's no question that Tessie's refusenik ways and even aggressive gestures toward owner Maude represent a dog taking the dominant role almost by force. Boomer was dominant-aggressive toward other dogs, with nothing playful about his lunges and occasional use of the mouth. Perhaps Hugo, our lovable bulldog, comes closest to Harley's situation, although Harley is more active by about times ten. Hugo was almost sucked into the dominant role as if by a vacuum. And that vacuum was the absence of effective leadership from the humans in Hugo's life.

Harley is in much the same boat. No one is showing effective leadership in Harley's life, and so he has taken a position of authority for himself, doing all he can to focus all attention on himself. And while he is not dominant in the way that Tessie was with Maude, or feels the need to be dominant to protect his owner, as Boomer did, his body language still reflects a strong attitude of dominance, with his tail often carried straight up in the air as he walks and a continuous attitude of playful challenge toward family members that ultimately allows him to do what he pleases. It's not simply that the family isn't saying "No"; they have no means of enforcing limits because Harley has no real understanding of the fundamentals. Further complicating matters is the fact that he is unneutered, something we not only note in our telephone interview, but will strongly suggest they address after he returns home.

Mary Ellen has spoken of "failing" on discipline, and we see signs of improperly handled correction in several interactions between Harley and people. Mary Ellen herself will repeat a strong "No" without getting any control over Harley's behavior, and she does compound the problem by throwing in Harley's name. We'll take yet another opportunity here to emphasize that a dog's name should never be associated with a correction, but only with a positive command, or with praise. You always want to be able to call your dog and have him come, so you never want him associating his name with anything negative. And just as important, repeating an ineffective correction can make it have an opposite effect. The "No" becomes an encouragement to further rambunctiousness on Harley's part, almost like a "Go." It's because it's a meaningless correction, with nothing behind it.

> "I have a really positive feeling
> it's going to make a big difference
> in his life, in our lives."
>
> —Mary Ellen

We also observe that even while they're complaining about Harley's boisterous ways, some of the friends that hang out with Chris and Rob are goading Harley to it, teasing him with little feint moves with their hands and the like. It's all for fun, but they're deliberately riling Harley up. They don't know how to stop what they start, but they're also giving Harley mixed messages about what's allowed.

Rob, the thirteen-year-old, has the tightest bond with Harley, and he does seem to have some measure of control over him. But we do notice something even here that may be key. Rob is the nicest kid you ever want to meet, quiet and thoughtful, with a warm heart and a gentle smile. We know he's worried about Harley and that's influencing his whole mood, but we also find he's remarkably patient with his dog, tolerating a great deal and then correcting with a soothing, quiet voice. He talks about having heard that it never does any good to lose your temper with a dog and yell at him. That is of course absolutely right.

But is Rob almost too patient with Harley? Is Rob the missing leader in Harley's life? Even though he's aware that Harley is annoying people and that his mom has seriously considered getting rid of him, Rob still professes, "He doesn't seem that annoying to me." His love runs almost dangerously deep with this dog—dangerous in the sense that he risks their relationship by letting Harley be dominant. Rob will need to learn, as will the whole family, that Harley needs to look to a leader and that Rob can learn to exercise this in a benevolent, helpful way that enhances the bond they share. This is a challenge that often faces children and their dogs, and Rob will need patient coaching to assume that role comfortably. Fortunately, he is big for his age and quite coordinated. That will stand him in good stead as he practices with Harley.

As for the mouthing behavior itself, we feel that's all part of the attention-seeking, dominant-dog package. It's Harley saying "Me, me, me!" To some degree it's a breed tendency from puppyhood that has become habitual, a pattern that will need to be stopped. Once he learns his proper place, and his family learns to give him attention in a more enriching way, we fully expect the mouthing will no longer be an issue.

WHAT IF tip

If your dog won't calm down no matter what—even if you run him ragged—you may have a clinically hyperactive dog. Some dogs are either born this way or reach a stage where their obstreperous behavior can't be turned off with commands alone. While this isn't nearly as common as some would believe and we would use medication only as a last resort, there are times when effective medications can address the problem and get your dog into a calmer state where training is possible. Talk to both a competent trainer and your veterinarian.

AT THE MONASTERY

As Mary Ellen drives up the last stretch of road to New Skete, Harley leans forward from the back seat and starts licking her neck. Mary Ellen says, "No, no, no, Harley, no licking. Stop." Harley keeps licking away. He's undoubtedly picking up the vibes of Mary Ellen's feelings as she brings him to us for a month of training. "He's a part of everything," she says. "Even with all the craziness, you don't know how you had a life without him." We know that son Rob will miss Harley even more. "It is really important to me that Brother Chris has come along," Rob told us earlier, "because I know Harley's going to get better." We think it's Rob's way of *not* saying how much he's going to miss his dog.

Brother Christopher's first meeting with Harley is a lesson in just how unmanageable this golden retriever can be. Harley jumps toward Brother Christopher, his paws hitting at waist level, and for a moment even the well-prepared Brother Christopher is almost knocked off his feet. Harley shows off his ability to grab his own leash and try to wrest it out of Mary Ellen's grip. He cavorts and prances and chews and, oh, by the way, won't obey any commands. Harley is a ball of golden fire, and no one has an extinguisher.

"The dog will sense in positive leadership someone who is worth listening to and following."

—Brother Christopher

Brother Christopher sees the process that lies ahead and only prevents Harley from jumping up again; he doesn't yet begin anything that could be classified as formal training, anything in the way of meaningful correction. Training and discipline always need a context, and he will establish that in the first days of the program. After questioning Mary

Ellen on what he sees in Harley's behavior and clarifying certain aspects of her family's experience with him, he allows Mary Ellen to say her goodbyes, then takes Harley to the kennels. When he returns, he answers several questions Mary Ellen has about the training process and explains the daily routine Harley will be subject to in learning the exercises.

We have encouraged the whole family to read our books while Harley is with us. Even *The Art of Raising a Puppy* will hold valuable information, since Harley is only a year old and the more they understand about canine development, the better. In more specific terms, though, we describe the dominance issue, and encourage Mary Ellen to prepare to take a more active role in Harley's training—not just Mary Ellen herself, but by all means the boys as well.

We point out that Harley clearly needs more exercise, that a lot of his rambunctiousness is just his effort to burn off steam. Golden retrievers really do need a very active life, with walks and vigorous games, and Harley has an absolute need for this in a daily, consistent manner. For example, a great game for Harley would be "fetch," getting a tennis ball and bringing it back repeatedly. But we emphasize even more that Harley needs someone to be the leader, to give him clear, consistent guidance on the limits of behavior and getting his obedience through a proper use of the training exercises.

We talk about the issue of indulgence, and how it is preventing their relationship with Harley from reaching its potential. The best example— and a point we want to make with Mary Ellen—has to do with the muzzle they've used with Harley when he's getting really out of control. The muzzle has calmed Harley down, and there's nothing inherently wrong with using one. We've even recommended them, especially when the owner needs to build up his or her confidence that an aggressive dog is under control. The point here is how guilty they all feel about using it. We represent this to Mary Ellen as a sign that perhaps they're not willing to be firm enough with Harley. We talk about Rob's patience, about a sometimes passive response to Harley's antics. Harley gets away with things, and that's only because all of them are letting him. While Rob might have the closest bond with Harley of the family members, we explain that since he is only thirteen he will need her support in achieving leadership which, while not impossible (and he clearly has both talent and interest), often requires the assistance of a parent to help it stick.

Most of all, we want to make clear to Mary Ellen that effective leadership is in the best interests of her primary goal, one she has mentioned more than once—of fully integrating Harley into their lives. We will guide her, and encourage her to learn more, about giving commands properly. And we reassure her that, once Harley knows the basics, if she and all the family will follow through, giving direction and showing leadership on a consistent basis, Harley will thrive.

HARLEY'S TRAINING

Isn't it interesting that we never get a dog with a specific behavioral problem—like Harley's mouthing—who is otherwise well-trained and obedient? We're being facetious, to make a point. Although we know that Harley has a mouthing behavior, and that we may ultimately have to take steps to break him of this habituated response, the most important focus of our training is basic obedience, because the lack of it is the root cause of the problem. Without being able to replace bad behavior with desired behavior that he understands, frustration will inevitably be the result. First we need to get Harley used to the concept of following direction, acknowledging leadership through teaching him the basic exercises, the bedrock of a successful relationship with a dog. Then, if necessary, we can fine-tune specific behaviors.

Harley is eager from the moment he gets out of the kennel into the exercise area. His head swivels from side to side as he scans for something to interact with. Brother Christopher plans nothing formal for the

Heel, come and down with Harley

Harley demonstrates three of the basics. He walks perfectly at heel, right beside Brother Christopher, who is holding the leash with the right amount of slack (1). From a sit, Harley eagerly heads for Brother Christopher in response to the come command (2). Harley holds the down-stay position, keeping his focus riveted on his handler (3).

first few days. He merely wants Harley to get used to him, to get used to the leash and training collar he's wearing, to familiarize himself with the surroundings and increase his comfort level. Brother Christopher will definitely start correcting inappropriate behavior, but he won't introduce Harley's first obedience command yet.

Brother Christopher keeps a loose hold on the leash; he wants Harley to try to take the lead so he can correct him. Some dogs stray into the lead, sniffing their way out to tugging range. There's nothing "stray" about Harley. He bounds out to the end of the leather leash, then turns and bounds back toward Brother Christopher. He starts to jump up, and Brother Christopher gives a quick, firm pop to the leash, at the same time saying a short, sharp "No!" He's not surprised by Harley's almost spastic-looking jumpiness. "It's common with golden retrievers," he says. "They're active, energetic dogs, and they're always going to try to assert dominance. Harley's doing it by trying to knock into me."

They work again at just walking along, and Brother Christopher corrects Harley with a leash pop and a quick change of direction every time he bounds out to the end of the leash. He wants Harley to see that he, Brother Christopher, is setting the direction and the pace— being the leader.

Harley begins to get the picture, but still seeks to get attention by mouthing at his own leash. To prevent this, Brother Christopher quickly jerks the leash straight up into Harley's mouth with a brusque "NO!" The metal clip on the leash knocks into the bottom of Harley's muzzle and Harley immediately lets go. As they continue to move forward Brother Christopher corrects jumping and straining on the leash with leash pops and quick changes of directions.

Within a few days, Harley is good enough at following Brother Christopher that he's ready to try heeling in a formal way. Going over the same, familiar ground, Harley is focused on Brother Christopher, who says "Heel" as they start out. Whenever Harley gets ahead—not as far as the end of the leash, but just ahead at all—Brother Christopher corrects and changes direction, then gives the heel command again. He praises Harley profusely in a light, higher-toned voice when he keeps to the heel position, right beside him.

Eye contact was initially a problem for Harley, but Brother Christopher has worked every session on getting him to pay attention to Brother Christopher's eyes, to maintain eye contact. He does this by encouraging Harley to look up at him with a "Watch me" while frequently pointing his finger up at his eyes, and praising him warmly when he does. The initial leash training, and now the heel command, have reinforced for Harley that he can best avoid correction by paying attention to Brother Christopher's every move. He's definitely understanding the concept of leader.

It's clear now that Harley is a smart dog, who can be very responsive and can even be quite calm in controlled circumstances. He is not clinically hyperactive at all (see "What If tip, page 199). And as the

Our Favorite—and Unfavorite—Things

We've already discussed the importance of exercise and free play, which we incorporate into the daily routine of our puppies here at New Skete. But what to play with? As we mentioned before, we start with a rolled-up newspaper to simulate a ball when the puppies are very small. But as they get older, and when they grow into adult dogs, they're ready for other playthings. We have our preferences, but we'd also like to warn you about some toys that may not be good for your dog.

Our favorite things include a flavored nylon chew bone, a plastic play ring you can toss, a sterilized bone, any of the widely available rubber toys into which you can insert treats, a rubber ball that's not too small for your dog, and ordinary rope toys. But here's where you need to be vigilant. Be sure to get rid of a rope toy once it becomes frayed; the loose strands are easy for your dog to swallow and have been known to cause internal blockages.

What don't we like? Stay away from tied-up socks, old shoes, squeak toys (which have small parts that your dog may be able to get to if the toy gets ripped open), and anything "stringy" that your dog could swallow. We also have a word of warning about some common standbys. A tennis ball can be a great toy for a dog of the right size, but if your dog is larger, he might get it stuck in his throat during excited play. As for rawhide bones, they're okay but only if you're around to supervise—and inter-

training time goes into the second week, Harley is picking up quickly on sit and moving right on to sit-stay.

Brother Christopher uses a little proofing trick to encourage Harley to stay in a sit. After putting him into the position with hand gesture and command, Brother Christopher steps back but keeps a steady, slight pressure on the leash. This actually causes Harley to lean back a little, resisting that slight pressure forward coming through the leash; it keeps his butt down on the ground in the sit-stay position.

They move on to down-stay, which will be a vital command for the family to rely on. After initially placing Harley into a down position manually (thus giving him a clear idea of what the command means), Brother Christopher starts to practice down from the sit, giving him the command and guiding him into a down position. In a matter of a couple of sessions Harley is going down willingly, without any sort of corrective pop and staying put for a couple of minutes. Gradually Brother Christopher extends the length of time Harley holds the down-stay position, adding distractions and challenges that increase his ability to stay in the position. With such a foundation, when Mary Ellen and the boys anticipate a situation where Harley might jump up—such as a bunch of kids coming into the house all in a big rush—they can put Harley into a down and hold him there until things in general calm down.

Remember These Things

It bears repeating: Never use your dog's name when giving correction.
Reinforce a sit-stay with slight pulling pressure on the leash.
Put your dog in down-stay if you anticipate he might jump up.

HARLEY TRANSFORMED

We're into the last phase of Harley's training, and Brother Christopher moves on to proof Harley's good behavior. "Training is a process," he says, "and you have to allow the dog a progressive possibility of making mistakes in increasingly distracting situations." So Brother Christopher begins by trying to distract Harley out of a down-stay by tossing his hat nearby. Harley lunges the first couple of times, but quick correction—Brother Christopher still has the leash in hand—soon solves the problem. Brother Christopher has also increasingly been giving Harley opportunities to try to mouth his hand or arm—but on Brother Christopher's terms. By taking the distraction to him, petting him around his face and muzzle as he is in the sit position, he's tempting Harley to put his mouth on his hands. If Harley does, Brother Christopher is ready with a brief, sharp tap on his snoot followed by an open hand that encourages him to lick. If he tries to mouth while walking, he gives Harley a quick leash correction and quickly makes several attention-getting roundabout turns.

Harley is still every bit the classic American dog loving life—but he's even more a part of the family.

But Harley doesn't take the bait. Brother Christopher now moves on to walking Harley past both strangers and acquaintances. A few times he has to be leash-corrected, but he understands what's expected very quickly. Brother Christopher even has someone come at Harley with an outstretched hand, hoping he can tempt Harley into mouthing and then

give him correction. Again Harley fails to fail. He seems to have understood, through the process of learning the basic obedience commands, that mouthing is no longer an acceptable form of interaction with people.

Mary Ellen and the boys come to pick up Harley after the four weeks, and from behind the glass they rave about how controlled and obedient he is. But he clearly still has every ounce of that lovable personality when they get to come out and greet him. Brother Christopher, during the time that he works with Mary Ellen and Rob and Chris on giving the basic commands correctly, reminds Rob of how important it is to play with Harley a lot, to give him plenty of opportunities to chase a ball and to run around. It's a good way to get him into a less-energized state for a training session, but we emphasize that it also has to be a pattern, combined with walks, of getting Harley enough exercise on a daily basis.

And of course we give our lecture—or should we say, our friendly talk—on the importance of leading Harley into good behavior, of anticipating problems, then replacing misbehavior with a clearly given command. Part of the secret is in focusing on doing positive things—giving obedience commands—before you have to get to the point of correcting negative behaviors. It's all about being a leader.

As Brother Christopher puts it, "The dog will sense in positive leadership someone who is worth listening to and following. I think the sooner that the owners accept that responsibility, the healthier their relationships with their dogs become."

Weeks later, sitting to greet visitors, no longer pouncing on guitars or grabbing cushions or chewing on sneakers to get attention, Harley has become much more involved in his family's daily life. Rob has taken the lead in daily training sessions that have created a nice transfer from the monastery to the home. There's still progress to be made, but clearly a great deal of improvement has already occurred. Harley's still fun, still every bit the classic American dog loving life—but he's even more a part of the family now that all its members know their appropriate roles.

Q&A: Training as Therapy

My dog has specific misbehaviors that are his only problems. Can I hire someone to train him out of those specific problem behaviors?

There's a major misconception among many dog owners that you can address problem behaviors only and skip "all that obedience stuff." Owners need to understand that there are no shortcuts: The essential prerequisite to solving any problem is always basic obedience training. It provides a context, a language through which you can communicate meaningfully with your dog.

Basic obedience training teaches your dog to respect you as a leader and to have confidence in your authority. Being your dog's leader may be new to you, especially if you've been indulgent in the past. But lack of clear direction from you may, in fact,

be the source of the problem you're facing. If you're serious about tackling problems, you need to be willing to make changes in your own behavior first.

A misbehavior that has become ingrained over time may still require the assistance of a qualified professional, who can indeed help you solve a specific problem. But never forget that you have to follow through. Work with the professional and learn what you need to do to reinforce the training and prevent backsliding. And always remember that being firm and consistent with your dog is what love really looks like.

My male dog's been aggressive with other dogs and growls at strangers sometimes. I'm worried that he's going to hurt someone. Is there anything I can do?

Is your dog neutered? Unneutered males tend to be more aggressive, so arrange to have him neutered as soon as possible. But this is only the first step. If you are familiar with training, immediately begin 15-minute

sessions twice a day on the basic commands, especially heel, sit and stay. For the time being, think preventively and avoid interactions with other dogs until you are in better control and can set up meetings safely. If your dog is aggressive toward visitors to your home, have him crated before anyone comes in. Allow him to see the visitor and settle down before you bring him out on leash, then use the proper "introduction" technique, bringing your dog up to the guest—the guest should never approach first—and having him sit and stay. Tell your guest to avoid eye contact initially, and speak naturally with your guest for a few minutes. Note your dog's body posture and general demeanor. If he is settled, allow him to sniff the back of your guest's hand, and praise him warmly for a polite response. Also, seriously consider getting professional help to assist you with all angles of this problem.

If this technique doesn't work, or if you have never trained before, get professional help as soon as possible. Don't procrastinate. Ask potential trainers about their experience with cases of aggression. Be honest about the problems you're having, and keep in mind that your own behavior and relationship with your dog may need some adjusting. Be open to constructive criticism.

My dog and I play tug-of-war and she loves it, but she growls up a storm. Should we give up our favorite game?

There's a difference of opinion among trainers about tug-of-war. Some feel it encourages possessiveness and aggression and can be particularly problematic for guarding breeds and high-energy dogs, who might go too far, with potentially serious consequences. Others believe it can promote bonding and can be a good way to burn up your dog's energy reserves.

Be honest in evaluating your own dog. Does she have any possession or aggression issues? If so, work on teaching her a less risky game like fetch. If you feel it's safe to play tug, keep the following things in mind. You as primary handler should be the only one to play the game, and under no circumstances should you let children be involved. Start teaching the game in puppyhood, when it's easiest to establish clear guidelines and set limits. Make sure you—and not your dog—are always the initiator. Teach the "release" and "give back" commands, as well as "time out" so you can stop the game if you sense your dog is starting to get too excited. Take possession of the tug toy and put it away when you've decided to end the game. This type of play always needs to be entirely on your terms.

The Basics

Sit ○
Heel ●
Stay ●
Down ●
Come ○

BONNIE

Defying the Odds

Sometimes dogs defy all the odds, surviving unimaginable cruelty and going on to lead full lives in kind and loving homes. Bonnie is one of those dogs—and then some. She has not just survived, but thrived, becoming a genuine working dog, out in the world interacting with people and other pets. Bonnie needs some touching-up on the basics, but she's really here to help us tell a story of what caring hearts can do in even the direst cases.

NOTE: *This chapter is different from every other in the book, because Bonnie is a different kind of dog, in lots of ways. She did not come to us as a "dog with a problem." But Bonnie did go through the same kind of training regimen here at the monastery as all the other dogs in this book, and she is an excellent example of how the principles of our approach work. She also teaches lessons about much, much more having to do with the interactions—of all kinds—between people and dogs. Besides all that, hers is a great story, full of love and hope and a host of other virtues.*

So we have broken the mold a bit and ventured away from some of the common features of other chapters—most noticeably the focus on "the problem" or other behavioral issues that need to be addressed. But you will get lessons aplenty from the story of this remarkable dog, and so we have chosen to let that story unfold in its own way.

loria has one of those jobs you don't hear about at Career Day in high school. She works as a representative for a natural pet foods company, traveling up and down the East Coast to pet stores and dog shows and other venues touting the benefits of her company's products, giving out samples, and otherwise preaching the advantages of good pet nutrition.

For years her constant companion and fellow "road warrior," as Gloria puts it, was a wonderful Airedale terrier named Lizzy, who was "trained to the nines." The first time Gloria took Lizzy with her on a demonstration, the effect was dramatic: People were stopping who normally would have walked by, and everyone wanted to pet Lizzy, who apparently took it all just perfectly.

Some connection leaped into Gloria's heart from the very first moment she laid eyes on Bonnie.

Sadly, Lizzy died of a relatively rare intestinal condition at the age of eight. Gloria went back to working on her own, but as she recalls, "people were walking right by again, and not paying attention again, and I just thought, oh this is not going to work." So she began the process of finding a new "demo dog."

Despite the fact that she has a light-hearted, self-deprecating manner, Gloria takes her work very seriously and she has every reason to feel proud of her own dedication. It shows in how she talks about her company, and it also shows in how she went about searching for a new dog. "I interviewed literally hundreds of dogs," she says, looking for very specific traits that work best in the meet-and-greet environment of being a demo dog. "I wanted a dog that looked non-threatening, and I wanted a dog that everybody could relate to," Gloria recalls. But her list of requirements was much longer than that. For one thing, a rescue dog was a must; it's an issue near and dear to her heart and it's also, frankly, a good way to stir passersby's interest. She needed a dog who would do well with strangers, with other dogs and other sorts of pets as well, who would obey commands unfailingly, who could travel well, and so on and so on.

After six months of searching, she still hadn't found the right combination of attributes, but she kept on trying, sticking to her rigorous standards. "I really could not afford to make a mistake," Gloria says.

And that's what makes Bonnie's part in the story all the more amazing. When Gloria saw a picture of Bonnie, "all the care I had taken with these hundreds of dogs went right out the window."

We have to stop and say that's not really true, that Gloria didn't really throw caution to the wind. But her words do indicate that something happened to her that day; some connection leaped into her heart from the very first moment she laid eyes on an image of Bonnie.

Gloria had been perusing a whole bunch of listings on petfinder.com, a well-known online database of homeless pets and rescue organizations. She noticed one group of rescues from the Oklahoma Animal Welfare Association and saw a photograph of Bonnie. "I don't know what it was about that picture," she says, "but there was something special there." She called the contact number and said to the woman on the other end of the line, "I want to know about this dog Bonnie."

BONNIE'S RESCUE

Bonnie was found during an investigation into a case of neglect that had been reported by a concerned citizen. She was being kept in a small wire pen along with several other large dogs, including huskies and St. Bernards; there were a total of sixteen dogs on the property, as well as sheep and goats, all of them underfed to the point of

All her front teeth were either gone
or broken, most likely from chewing
on the wiring of her far-too-small pen.

malnourishment. Some of the dogs were in cages like Bonnie's, and others were chained. There was no clean water available, and the caged animals were living in what seemed to be months' worth of feces. Some of the dogs were too far gone to rescue.

Bonnie is a mix of Airedale and Great Pyrenees and should have weighed about 75 pounds; she tipped the scales at only 37 pounds when she was rescued. All her front teeth were either gone or broken, most likely from chewing on the metal wiring of the far-too-small pen where she clearly spent all her time. She had gnawed on one of her legs, creating a hotspot, tested positive for a serious tick-borne disease called ehrlichia, and had a raging ear infection.

Bonnie and the others were victims of animal hoarding. It's a recognized psychological condition that you may have heard about on the news. Hoarders seem well-intentioned, at least at first, but they can't control their urge to collect more and more animals, even when they no longer care for the ones they already have. Some cat hoarders have been found keeping literally hundreds of cats in unimaginably deplorable circumstances.

The Oklahoma Animal Welfare Association took possession of Bonnie and promptly got her most serious afflictions treated. She had surgery to repair her dental problems, although she did end up losing her canines and all her front bottom teeth. Antibiotics were prescribed for the ehrlichia. The ear infection and hotspot were less immediate concerns that proper nutrition would help address. So her rescuers also got her back onto a reasonable diet.

And then along came Gloria.

BONNIE'S NEW HOME

After hearing all about Bonnie and asking a ton of questions, Gloria took the plunge and decided to adopt Bonnie. That's what she means about throwing all the care out the window: Instead of seeing Bonnie face-to-face first, Gloria went ahead and made the commitment. She trusted in that connection she had felt from the picture. "Even if she didn't work out as a demo dog," she recalls thinking, "there was no way I was giving up on Bonnie."

Bonnie was flown from Oklahoma, and Gloria picked her up in a cargo hangar at an airport about forty-five minutes from her home in New Jersey. After the car drive home, Gloria let Bonnie out in her back-yard, not knowing what to expect. "But from the moment she stepped out of that crate," Gloria recalls, "everything seemed perfect." Bonnie was friendly and affectionate, if somewhat tentative at the very first. She didn't seem fearful, and there was no whimpering or needy behavior. She was remarkably trusting, given the kind of treatment she'd had— although it should be said that she had never been actively physically abused or beaten.

Perhaps most important of all, Gloria noticed right away that Bonnie had "the kindest eye. The only word I can use to describe her is 'gracious.'" Again, after all she had been through, it was quite astounding.

There were, naturally enough, a few adjustments. Having apparent-ly always lived outside, Bonnie had to be housebroken; it took all of two days. She was unfamiliar with lots of indoor things, including stairs, which just didn't seem to make any sense to her. She was afraid of the roar of the vacuum cleaner and hair dryer at first, but she got used to them relatively quickly. Her reaction to such foreign elements in her world never devolved into the kind of behaviors we've seen in other dogs—like Sweet Puppy's attacking of the broom.

Gloria did notice that Bonnie was a little insecure, always wanting to

"The only word I can use to describe
her is 'gracious'".

—Gloria

BONNIE:
"This person really cares about me."

GLORIE:
"I can't believe what a sweet dog she is!"

THE MONKS:
"Bonnie is a dog to learn from. She has a special spirit, and a joy in life. We see it in other dogs as well, and we always look for it and expect it; then we are always ready to nurture it or help establish it when it needs help."

keep Gloria in her sights and when they were together always putting her paw on Gloria as if to say, "Don't forget I'm here." She also didn't have any idea what play was about, just didn't get it when Gloria would throw her a ball or a stick and try to get her some exercise that way. And it was pretty obvious that she hadn't had any obedience training of any kind. Minor issues in the larger scheme of things, as far as Gloria was concerned. She still had every confidence that Bonnie was the right choice.

In a surprisingly short space of time, Gloria felt ready to test the waters of what she hoped and expected would be Bonnie's new career. They set out for a typical venue—a pet store.

Gloria couldn't have been more pleased with the results. The big, lovable, furry, cuddly thing that she is, Bonnie was a natural magnet for dog lovers of every stripe. She did tend to interact a little too playfully with other dogs, willing or not, and she occasionally jumped up toward people, straining on the leash—all well-intentioned, with not a trace of aggression or dominance to it, but not quite the perfect behavior that would be required over the long haul. All in all, though, it was an entirely positive test. There was no longer any shadow of a doubt in Gloria's mind that Bonnie would be her new "road warrior."

Like the good dog owner she is, Gloria then let Bonnie settle in for a few more days before giving her any training. It didn't take long until Bonnie was relaxing more and more. And then one day, Gloria noticed a subtle but important difference. "It was as if a light bulb had gone off," Gloria says, "and she was thinking, 'Hey, this is a cool place to be.'"

Gloria then decided to begin training Bonnie. Yet one more thing that sets Bonnie's story apart from the others in this book is that Gloria is an accomplished trainer, well versed in the proper techniques. So she knew all about how to introduce Bonnie to the basic obedience commands. And in short order Bonnie learned how to sit, stay, heel, come and lie down.

What Bonnie Needed

Gloria was extremely pleased with the results of testing Bonnie in the "demo dog" environment and equally happy about the quick progress she made with basic commands. But she knew Bonnie still needed some work. "A demo dog has to be rock-solid" on the commands, Gloria says, "and I have to be able to trust her 200 percent." Dog trainers call this "proofing" the commands—ensuring that they will be obeyed in every circumstance, no matter what. This would be particularly important for Bonnie, who could expect to be prodded and poked by children, have her ears pulled and played with, and the like.

Gloria fully intended to do this proofing herself, somehow or other given her busy schedule. But then one more fortuitous event occurred—and that's where we at New Skete come into the picture.

Unrelated to Bonnie's situation, we had arranged a meeting with some of the managers at Gloria's company, and Gloria was offered the chance to come to the meeting as well, with Bonnie. It would give her a chance to

Goals for Bonnie
- Become more confident
- "Proof" basic obedience commands
- Improve eye contact
- Enlarge her circle of trust

introduce her great new find to some of her superiors. Plus, she had heard about our work and was anxious to meet us—and, she admits, show off this remarkable dog who had survived such horrible neglect and come through with flying colors.

AT THE MONASTERY

On a bright, warm day in early spring, Gloria and Bonnie arrived at New Skete, and we instantly fell in love with this big wonderful shaggy dog. Brother Christopher met Bonnie in the same area where we always have our introductions, and she displayed all the uncontrolled exuberance of a dog in the early stages of training: breaking the sit Gloria had put her in, fidgeting around, and at one point jumping up on Brother Christopher. Nothing too extreme, and only to be expected in the circumstances. What caught our attention more was how full of joy and affection this dog was, and we could see that same kindness in the eye Gloria had noticed from day one. Frankly, we were looking for any signs of compulsive behavior or any other aftereffects of the terrible treatment she had suffered. There was only the hotspot on her leg, and those missing teeth. Behaviorwise, she seemed normal in every regard.

After the "business" part of our meeting, we came to a quick decision—it was an easy one—and told Gloria that we would like to offer her the opportunity to have Bonnie trained by Brother Christopher here at the monastery. She was thrilled, and we made arrangements on the spot for her to bring Bonnie back to us in a few weeks' time.

BONNIE'S TRAINING

When Bonnie arrives at New Skete to begin her month of training, we spend an hour or so talking with Gloria about the goals of training. We know that Gloria doesn't need instruction on giving obedience commands, and we can see as the two of them walk around the exercise area that Bonnie has a basic understanding of all five exercises. We also note how calm and friendly she is, that she shows no signs of fear aggression or compulsive behavior, and that she has continued to recover. Her gorgeous coat is clean and well-groomed, she is back up to the normal weight for the type of dog she is, and the hair is beginning to grow back over the hotspot on her left rear thigh. Brother Christopher marvels: "This was a real rescue. I haven't seen a dog with a similar background recover like this. On the basis of her recovery alone, Bonnie is a very unusual dog."

We do notice one thing that may trace back to her mistreatment: She does not make good eye contact. When Brother Christopher takes

1

2

"I can honestly say that she is one of the
easiest dogs I've worked with in memory.
She is bright and happy—a real pleasure."

—Brother Christopher

Bonnie shows her stuff

Bonnie looks up eagerly at Brother Christopher as he praises her for holding a sit-stay (1). He gives the down command and motions her into the position with a hand gesture (2). Having told Bonnie to stay, Brother Christopher moves away and paces back and forth, holding her with a hand gesture alone (3); note how Bonnie keeps looking at him but doesn't break the down. Still reinforcing the command with a hand gesture, Brother Christopher is able to step over Bonnie (4) without distracting her out of position.

her out for her first session, he notes a mild insecurity on her part; when she senses that she may have made a mistake or done something wrong, she turns her head away and looks off to the left. "It was as though she was afraid to be a dog," Brother Christopher comments, "afraid that in making mistakes she might lose her new situation." He realizes he is projecting a human emotion onto Bonnie—something he often warns owners not to do—but throughout the training period he feels this strongly, that Bonnie continues to harbor a level of insecurity. It seems to fade almost day by day, but it never quite leaves her.

There is, of course, no way to say directly to a dog that she needn't worry about her future, that she has found a permanent loving home. All we can do is show her by consistent treatment, continual kindness, and a clear communication of expectations that her new life is something she will be able to rely on. Only time will cement that understanding in her.

Brother Christopher works with Bonnie on all the commands, and he finds her extremely easy to train. He keeps the pace moving at a nice clip to stimulate her interest. Working on heel, she needs very few corrections before she's doing it solidly and consistently. Sit is no problem at all. The one exercise that proves a bit challenging for her is stay. Brother Christopher is able to put her in a sit-stay or a down-stay with little difficulty, but she tends to break after a minute and wander off.

Remember These Things

- Find out as much as you can about a rescued dog.
- Make a thorough vet check your first priority.
- Be tolerant of misbehaviors initially.
- Don't be afraid to be firm when training begins, so long as you've established a preliminary level of trust.

The solution is the standard one. Brother Christopher uses the leash to give her a mild pop, accompanied by a verbal correction, whenever she starts to break a stay. Slowly, session by session, he is able to extend the time that he can leave her in the stay, and as she gets better and better he introduces distractions—stepping over her as she stays in the down position, or tossing a ball or his hat in her vicinity. Bonnie improves almost every time. It's a crucial part of the training, because obviously Gloria will often need to have Bonnie sit or lie down quietly while she makes a presentation, and the world around her will be full of distractions in all sorts of forms.

Eye Contact

From the first session on, Brother Christopher works hard at improving Bonnie's eye contact. He does this mostly from the sit-stay. Moving out in front of her to the length of the leash, he points up to his eyes and says brightly "Watch here!" After just a few seconds of eye contact, he deliberately looks away, breaking off the eye contact before she does. Then moving back and forth he repeats the command every so often, pointing to his eyes and keeping his voice light and pleasant and very encouraging. He holds the contact only for a short time and never engages in extended staring. The goal is to get her to look consistently when commanded—and as the lessons progress, so does her ability to keep focused on Brother Christopher.

The best part is that she is clearly becoming more and more comfortable making eye contact. This is a key ingredient to a deepening relationship between her and anyone working with her. She already has a strong bond with Gloria, but now she is showing signs of extending her circle of trust to someone else, in this case Brother Christopher. Those lingering signs of insecurity are continuing to fade.

Bonnie's Progress

Everything is going excellently with Bonnie. She's getting more reliable with all the commands. "Come" seems to be her specialty. Whether over a short or long distance, she comes right to Brother Christopher every time, ignoring all sorts of distractions he has arranged off to the side.

Bonnie also is becoming more affectionate and relaxed with strangers. It's a good sign of her continuing recovery, but occasionally it does go too far, to the point where she jumps up. So Brother Christopher stages some interactions at our gift shop, bringing her up to strangers in a controlled situation where she makes a move to jump up and Brother Christopher can immediately correct her with a leash pop. As with everything else, Bonnie gets the point fairly quickly.

The end of her training time is fast approaching, and Brother Christopher continues to be amazed. "I can honestly say that she is one of the easiest dogs I've worked with in memory. She is bright and happy—a real pleasure." You almost have to go back to the pictures of how she looked when she was rescued to realize where this dog has come from. "Bonnie is a walking testimony to the fact that a lot of dogs in shelters can become wonderful pets if they get the right attention and retraining," Brother Christopher notes.

He does find that she has started to become a little bored with the standard training, so in the last week he begins to do some preliminary off-leash training with her. They make some progress, but Bonnie's focus occasionally wanders, and sometimes she lags behind Brother Christopher, perhaps because she is still a little unsure of what's being asked of her. We will recommend to Gloria that she continue to work on this.

As for play, well, it's just not something Bonnie seems to understand. This is not unusual for dogs raised in puppy mills or who were otherwise neglected early in life. If they were not played with as puppies, it can be extremely difficult for them to pick up the notion later in life. But it's a relatively minor concern. Play is really just important as an additional form of exercise. Brother Christopher compensates by taking her on long walks unrelated to the training sessions themselves.

Gloria comes to pick up Bonnie, and Brother Christopher follows the same routine as with all the *Divine Canine* dogs. Gloria is impressed, especially with Bonnie's ability to hold eye contact. They have the typical ecstatic reunion, and it's good to see how strong their bond is. When it's time for them to leave, Bonnie does something she hasn't done before: She licks Brother Christopher's hand. It is a special, touching moment for all of us. The simplest of gestures, but it says in no uncertain terms that this dog who has every reason to be insecure—this amazing, wondrous dog—has learned to trust more and more.

BONNIE GOES TO WORK

Just a couple of days after Bonnie leaves us, we hear from Gloria. Things are going better than great. Gloria had not planned to start working with Bonnie right away, but a friend who does fundraising for the American Cancer Society made a special appeal: Could Gloria bring Bonnie to a fundraising event? She thought Bonnie might be just the draw she needed. Gloria and Bonnie showed up the next day, and Bonnie worked her magic. Lots of kids came up to her, petting her, hugging her, and in the case of one little child who went too far, giving her a couple of smacks. "Bonnie sat there with all the grace and dignity of a queen," Gloria reports proudly. She also lets us know that her friend raised more money that day than in the previous six.

We can't say we're surprised. Bonnie is a charmer, and her story is as heartwarming as they get. We would be pleased to see *any* dog in such loving, competent hands as Gloria's. But for it to be Bonnie, whose suffering at the hands of humans is hard for us to grasp—that just makes it all the more wonderful. Against all the odds, Bonnie has taught us all how far the miracle of loving relationships can take us.

Bonnie's is a great story, full of love and
hope and a whole host of other virtues.

Q&A:
Life with Your Dog

I like to have my dog with me all the time, and that's what she's used to. Is it possible to travel with my dog, including air trips? Should I leave her with a sitter or is kenneling okay?

We have always encouraged owners to travel with their dogs whenever possible. Current airline regulations make flying with a dog difficult, though, and some airlines have discontinued pet travel entirely, save for assistance dogs. Check with individual airlines and do so as early in your plans as possible since even if an airline takes dogs, space will be limited.

For car trips, condition your puppy to the experience early on. Take fun trips that end on a happy note—with a walk in a new place, say, rather than a visit to the veterinarian. Once your dog is comfortable, you're ready for longer trips. Use a crate or some form of safety restraint, and never let your dog out without leashing him first. Stop every couple of hours to let him stretch and go to the bathroom, and always be conscientious about cleaning up after him. Ahead of time, make sure to locate dog-friendly lodging. Some hotels charge an additional fee for dogs and ask for a deposit in case of damage.

If you can't take your dog with you, it's perfectly reasonable to leave him in a kennel. Ask your veterinarian or friends for recommendations, and check the kennel out beforehand. Look for cleanliness and pleasantness of atmosphere first. Inquire about additional services such as daily exercise or training. We have found that periodic kenneling can actually help some dogs mature and become more independent and flexible.

Pet sitting provides more personalized care and is often less stressful for your dog. Seek recommendations, check credentials (only use licensed and insured sitters), and evaluate the pet sitter ahead of time; both you and your dog need to feel comfortable. Confirm what services the sitter will provide, and be sure they include daily exercise.

Our dog is getter older. We'd like to bring another dog into our lives as soon as possible. Should we wait, or is it okay to bring a new dog into our old dog's life?

There are real advantages to bringing a new dog into your home while your first dog is still healthy enough to enjoy a companion. A new puppy often rejuvenates an older dog by stimulating activity and play, but so can a new adult dog. So long as you don't show a preference for the new arrival, most dogs without dog-aggression problems will adapt easily to the presence of another dog in the house. Just be certain to build and maintain a bond with each dog individually.

Introduce the two dogs properly, preferably at a neutral location off your home property. (See pages 44-45 for more information.) If you take the trouble to let your older dog get used to the new dog gradually, you will likely see them become fast friends. But you should always be sensitive to your older dog's needs. If you bring a puppy into your home, make sure you give plenty of attention to your older dog during the first days so that the older dog does not feel excluded. Also, don't let the puppy "terrorize" the older dog with more demands for play than the older dog can accommodate. Use the crate to teach the pup to chill out and rest. Pups need lots of rest anyway,

and these periods will also give you and your older dog some quality one-on-one time. You can also expect a certain amount of legitimate "disciplining" from the older dog, who will likely want to demonstrate his position of primacy in the "pack" and make sure the newcomer understands her place. Don't try to stop this so long as neither dog is getting hurt.

A new pup introduced and raised correctly can bring a lot of joy to the family and to your older dog. We suggest reading—or re-reading—our book *The Art of Raising a Puppy* and applying those guidelines to the complete training of your younger dog.

MASTER CLASS

The Basics
- **Sit**
- **Heel**
- **Stay**
- **Down**
- **Come**

Teaching Your Dog the Basic Commands

Throughout this book, you've seen a variety of dogs—with a variety of behavioral issues—become transformed through the process of learning the basic obedience commands. Some dogs needed work on one command more than others; some had two or three they had to learn; and some were virtual blank slates, with no previous training in any of the commands. We chose to emphasize, in step-by-step illustrations, specific commands that were particularly significant for each individual dog.

Now, though, we'd like to go through all the basics of obedience training in one place. This "master class" will give you clear guidance on each of the five basic commands—sit, heel, stay, down and come—and will illustrate the proper response from your dog. Whereas the earlier chapters sometimes showed a dog *not* getting it right, here you will primarily see both handler and dog going through the exercises as they should be performed and as they should look. You'll find here all the basic training information you'll need to lay a firm and effective foundation with your own dog—and, in the process, you'll meet a few other wonderful dogs who have gone through the New Skete residency training program.

Before we begin, though, we'd like you to keep a couple of things in mind. First and foremost, remember that whether the training succeeds or not depends on you. Before you begin any training session with your dog, read this chapter through several times and reflect on your own level of confidence. If you're a little unsure, which is entirely natural, spend a few moments thinking positively about the training and understand that mistakes will be an organic part of the process—both for you and for your dog. Don't allow that prospect to paralyze you. Visualize the exercises going well. It's vitally important that you communicate confidence to your dog.

With that confidence should come a sense of leadership. As we've emphasized throughout the book, being an effective leader for your dog is the key to making the training work. And it's an essential component to addressing any problem behaviors that might arise later.

When your dog sees you as the leader, coupled with your growing training skills, you will be able to ensure that your dog will obey you no matter what sorts of distractions may be present.

Finally—and we have of course said this already, several times—remember that training is a lifelong experience, and that it involves your entire relationship with your dog. That relationship will continue to grow and flourish throughout your dog's life if you keep this in mind. We would even hazard to say that every interaction you have with your dog is an opportunity to strengthen your relationship—to learn and to grow. You will find occasions for training in all aspects of your life together, not just within the parameters of formal obedience training. By all means work on the obedience basics formally and regularly—they do need to be reinforced continually. But also look for those other occasions every day for integrating the training into your daily life. Continue to teach, and to learn, throughout your years together.

The Basics on the Basics

Call this general principles, if you will—a few basic matters that apply to all the obedience commands. We'll briefly discuss the whens and wheres of lessons and give you a few things to keep in mind as you go through the specific drills. Check yourself every once in a while to be sure you're following these guidelines.

First, try to establish a regular schedule for formal training sessions. If you can do it at least once every day—but better twice a day, as we do in our residency program here at New Skete—especially with a completely untrained dog, that's terrific. Stick to a schedule that works for you and be patient with the process. Dogs may not be able to read calendars or tell time to the hour, but they do develop a sense of when to expect training—and if you've made it a positive experience, they'll be eager and in a good state of mind for learning.

Be aware that you'll make significantly more progress if you do a couple of shorter training sessions every day rather than one long one. Also, during the period your dog is learning the basic exercises, you need to practice *every* day rather than every other day, or once a week, or "if I get a free moment."

When you're training your dog yourself, it's best to exercise your dog before beginning a training session. This helps burn off excess energy that might cause your dog to be easily distracted. So go for a walk first, or play a game of fetch—not emphasizing any obedience part of the game but just letting the dog run as much as possible without getting totally tired. Be aware of the temperature and level of sunlight, realizing that training at midday or when it's really hot can quickly cause the dog to tire and lose focus. As for the session itself, keep it relatively short, no more than fifteen or twenty minutes. You can work on one command or more than one, but if you're doing several, drill each of them two or three times at the very least. The right kind of repetition (we'll discuss the wrong kind in a moment) really helps obedience sink in.

Choose a location for training, and try to have most of your initial lessons there. There's nothing wrong with giving a few obedience commands when you're out on a longer walk, wherever you happen to be that's appropriate, but you should also have one place in particular where you both can concentrate on having a lesson. Make sure it's somewhere with minimal distractions—not beside a busy road, for example. We use both paved and grassy areas, with lots of room to do long recalls.

During a lesson, remember to keep your command-giving voice upbeat, clear, confident, and encouraging. Use higher tones for praise. Your dog associates the higher register with the happy sound of his puppy littermates. Use lower tones for correction; this is analogous to the warning growl your dog's mother would have given to the litter. Avoid any kind of nagging or whining tone: Don't *beg* your dog to obey you. Issue a command and always follow through.

When you're giving a so-called active command, one that requires some action like sitting or heeling, say your dog's name first and then the command to establish a positive association. With the passive command to stay, when you're asking your dog *not* to do something, just use the command without the name. *Never* use your dog's name with "No" or any other form of correction. You don't want to associate the name with anything negative.

Now, about the "wrong" kind of repetition: If your dog doesn't respond to a command right away, don't fall into the bad habit of repeating the command multiple times. This only teaches your dog that she can decide whether to obey or not—that is, that she is the leader. Say the command, and if you don't get the correct response, make an immediate correction with a "No." Reset your position with the dog if you need to, and start over. Just avoid multiple repetitions.

There are three distinct steps to giving a correction:
- Give a quick leash pop, accompanied by a clipped "No" or sharp "Eh!"
- Give the command again, in an upbeat, encouraging tone.
- Praise your dog, using high tones, when she responds correctly to the command.

To do the leash pop properly, be sure the leash is slightly slack first. Give the quick pop to the leash, bringing it taut momentarily, then releasing the tension immediately. It's important not to pull or tug on the leash, which only encourages your dog to resist and to pull away from you. The point is to interrupt what your dog is doing incorrectly and focus her attention back on you. Then your dog will be receptive to hearing the command again.

Now we're ready to go through the five basic commands and how some of them are used in combination.

SIT

Zeus, a German shepherd, demonstrates the ideal sit position. Note the position of Brother Christopher's hands on the leash, prepared to give a leash pop if necessary.

SIT-STAY
Brother Christopher keeps Zeus in a sit by holding the leash high (1). Telling Zeus to stay,
he points to his eyes to keep Zeus's attention and steps back, keeping the leash slack (2).

Sit

We know very few dog owners who haven't at least tried this most basic of commands. It's a relatively simple one to get your dog to obey, and it's something you can begin to teach very early in a dog's life, before you begin formal obedience training.

There are a few tried-and-true ways to get a dog to sit. If you're working with a young puppy, start by getting her attention as you stand in front of her, jangling keys, snapping your fingers, or holding a ball or a favorite toy in your hand. When the puppy looks up at your hand, move it to a position slightly above her head; as she follows your hand, she'll naturally go into a sitting position. Say the word "Sit" and then give her lots of praise. If she doesn't sit but just looks at your hand, give a slight tap to her rear end to encourage her to sit. Again, say the com-

mand and give her praise when she does it. Don't force your dog into the sit by pushing down on her back at the rear end. You're conditioning her to associate her own action of sitting with the spoken command; that's why you ideally want her to do the sitting all by herself, with only the slightest of enticement with the gentle tap of your finger if necessary.

If your older dog has never had any kind of obedience training, or if your puppy still isn't getting the concept, you will need to guide him into his first sit. Crouch down beside your dog, on his right side facing forward. Place your right hand on his chest, above his front legs. Now place your left hand on his back at the shoulders, and smoothly stroke your hand down the length of his back, continuing over the tail and down to the back of the

LET'S GO

Brother Christopher takes Zeus on a controlled walk. The leash is slack, and Zeus has a certain amount of freedom to explore his environment.

HEEL

Brother Christopher begins a formal heel with Rex, an Airedale, by putting him in the sit position and praising him (1). He says "Heel" and they set off, with Rex's right shoulder even with Brother Christopher's left knee (2). Note the position of Brother Christopher's left hand on the leash, ready to give a quick leash pop for correction (3).

legs. As you say the command to sit, put pressure on the chest with your right hand and tuck the back legs into a sit with your left hand. As he is moving into the sit position, say the command and praise him warmly.

Once your dog understands the concept of sitting, you'll be able to start getting him to do it on command. Say your dog's name, followed by the command. If you wish, you can use a treat to make the transition from placing your dog into the sit by raising the treat from nose level upwards at a 45-degree angle. But be sure to wean him from this quickly by replacing the treat with a similar movement of your hand up above his head as you say the command. Praise warmly. Be ready to give slight pressure to his rear end if he doesn't comply. Finally, working with your dog on the leash, stand with the dog on your left, both of you facing in the same direction. Say the name and the command, gently lifting

the leash with your right hand and, if you need to, giving gentle pressure on the dog's back at the rear end.

You'll be incorporating sit into several other commands, so it's a good idea to have it well-learned. You can, however, teach sit after teaching heel.

Heel

Some people wrongly think of heel as a kind of specialty command, something that's really important for, say, dog-show dogs but not a necessary part of the average canine's lexicon. On the contrary, we believe heel is one of the most important commands for your dog to learn, one that demonstrates better than any of the others that you are the leader, someone to be listened to and, quite literally, followed. It's so crucial that we typically teach it first in formal obedience training, even before sit.

Starting with "Let's Go"

Before you begin to teach the formal heel command, you need to familiarize the dog with following your lead as you walk him on the leash. And to do that, you need to know how to hold the leash properly.

Working with a six-foot leash and your preferred training collar (see pages 140-141), stand on your dog's right side, facing forward, and attach the leash to the collar, ensuring that the collar is snug and sitting high on your dog's neck. Loop your right thumb through the handle part of the leash and let it lie across your palm. Making a fist, use the first two fingers of your right hand to grasp the leash about a quarter of the way down; lay your right hand against your right thigh, near the waist. Now grab the leash near its other end, about two-thirds of the way down, with your left hand, knuckles facing forward, and lay your hand against your left thigh, at about the same height as your right hand. You're now in the starting position, one that gives you the ability to make quick leash-pop corrections.

You're ready to go. Say your dog's name and then "Let's go!" in an animated tone, perhaps slapping your left thigh a couple of times for encouragement. Keep the leash slack—this is vitally important—and give your dog a certain amount of freedom to sniff the ground. You're not looking for her to be in the heel position, right by your side, just yet. But you are looking for an opportunity to give her a correction if she gets too far afield or starts to pull.

As you walk along, loosen your grip enough on the leash to let it extend to its full length. Before the leash goes taut—either because your dog is trailing behind or has surged ahead—give a quick, short pop to the leash as you say a "No" or "Eh!" and then immediately release the tension. Then, right away, make a change of direction; you can take a right-angle turn or better yet if your dog is ahead of you, turn in the exact opposite direction. Say the command again brightly, slap your thigh, and carry on, praising her as she follows you. Use only enough force to get your dog's attention. Your goal is to have the dog see you out in front, as the one leading the direction in which you're walking, no matter what that direction is.

WATCH ME

Brother Christopher ensures that
Nella, a fox-colored Labrador, stays
focused by pointing to his eyes and
saying "Watch me" during a heel.

STAY

Brother Christopher tells Birgitta,
a Dalmatian, to watch him (1),
then tells her to stay with the verbal
command and a hand gesture (2).

Practice this form of informal heeling, also called controlled walking, until you're confident that your dog gets the point that you set the agenda on walks, that you determine where you both are going—that you are, in a word, the leader.

The formal heel

Now you're ready for the formal version of heel. First, though, a quick word to reinforce that the formal heel is not just for the show ring. Granted, when you take a walk you won't do the whole of it on a formal heel, but a good portion of it will be, especially if you live in an urban or suburban environment. By alternating formal heeling with less-formal controlled walking, you still give your dog an opportunity to explore the environment and do his business while at the same time being able to go into a formal heel immediately, as for example, when you're walking on a busy street or you encounter another owner and dog—or whenever you want to have close control over him.

From the starting position with your dog to your left and your hands positioned properly on the leash, begin by making eye contact, saying "Watch me!" and pointing to your own eyes. Then say her name and give the com-

mand "Heel," and start walking briskly. Your goal now is to have her right by your side, her right shoulder even with your left leg.

She will undoubtedly not hold exactly to that position, even if she's already mastered the controlled walk. So when she starts to lag a little or get a little ahead, give her a leash pop and a verbal correction, then praise her warmly when she falls back into line beside your left leg. Reverse directions several times to make sure you have her attention, praising her warmly as she follows.

Let's go through the proper leash pop for this correction. It should be done with the left hand. Start with the leash slightly slack, then use your left hand to "pop" the leash (sideways or up depending on circumstances) with a short, quick motion, and then immediately release the tension on the leash. Again, never yank or tug on the leash or maintain the tension. Your goal is a short, quick, attention-getting corrective action, immediately followed by praise when your dog responds.

As you walk, make this quick pop simultaneous with a "No" whenever your dog is not in the proper position,

changing direction quickly and following the correction with encouraging praise as your dog responds. Remember, the correction is to regain your dog's attention, at which point she will be focused on the praise for being in the right place at the right time.

In the show ring, when a dog is at heel the handler is not permitted to give any praise. But we're not in the ring, so we do suggest that you talk encouragingly to your dog whenever she is holding to the heel. Don't make it too profuse, but you'll help keep her attention on what she's doing right with gentle praise along the way.

As we've indicated, it's important to work changes of direction into the heel. They reinforce leadership. In your initial lessons, it's a good idea to prepare your dog for a change in direction by saying something to her like, "Ok, we're going to turn now. Ready? Here we go..." You might even try "Watch me now" or something like that to help focus your dog's attention. Then, just before you turn, say her name and the command "Heel" and follow it up with warm praise.

Keep using the command with every turn in your

DOWN

From the sit position with Birgitta's attention focused (1), Brother Christopher gives the down command and brings his hand down to the ground in a dramatic gesture (2). Her body follows his hand down (she has previously been given a treat during this routine), and he finishes the command with the hand gesture for "Stay" (3).

early training sessions to reinforce the obedience and keep your dog focused. Eventually you should be able to turn in any direction—to the right, to the left, or in a 180-degree turn—and have your dog stay in the heel position.

The automatic sit

The well-trained dog will end every heel by going into a sit automatically, without you having to say or do anything except come to a stop. You want to teach your dog this because it has practical value in real-world situations. When you're on a walk and meet a friend, you want your dog to be at his best controlled behavior, ensuring that he won't jump up and can be greeted in a calm atmosphere.

Start teaching the automatic sit by coming to a stop shortly after turning to the right; your dog's momentum as he moves around you in the turn makes it easier to glide him into the sitting position. Hold the leash with your right hand as you stop, lifting up on it ever so slightly, and be ready to initially reach down with your left hand and gently touch your dog's rear end as you say his name and the sit command. You can also use a treat to encourage him to sit, but as we've said before, we suggest using treats only sparingly—intermittently. In any event, praise your dog when he moves into the sit. If he doesn't, give a quick, short correction and then follow with praise.

After about a week or ten days of daily training and numerous repetitions, your dog should be going into the sit as soon as you say the command, at which point you can start trying it by saying his name, but without giving the command at all. When you begin on the automatic sit, make your stop very precise and deliberate, sending a clear signal, then praise or correct and praise

DOWN-STAY

Having put Zeus in a down-stay, Brother Christopher is able to step back and forth over him without Zeus breaking the stay. A dog who is able to ignore this form of distraction has mastered the command.

as necessary. Finally, when you are ready, delete his name as well. Run through this several times per training session, and be consistent: Require that your dog go into the sit every time.

Stay

You're halfway to "Stay" when you've mastered "Sit." In fact, you will sometimes see the stay command described as a sit-stay. There's also a down-stay, about which you'll learn shortly.

You'll use a demonstrative hand signal at first to introduce your dog to staying. Have your dog sit to your left, holding the leash in your left hand. Keep slight pressure on the leash to help hold your dog in the sit position. Then bring your right hand down in a sweeping gesture,

stopping it right in front of your dog's nose as you say "Stay." Remember, don't use her name since you are asking her *not* to do something. Your palm should be open and your fingers together. As you say the command, step out with your right foot so that you can turn and face your dog. Keep your hand in front of your dog's face and the leash under tension for several seconds, then praise lavishly as you move back beside her.

Keep working on the stay, including the hand gesture, as you extend the time you hold her in the stay. Make it not more than fifteen or so seconds at first, then slowly lengthen the time. Don't be too ready to drop the leash completely; you want to be able to give a well-timed leash correction even when you're holding her in the stay longer and moving farther away from her should she need it. At first, just move to the length of the six-foot

SIT-STAY-COME

Brother Christopher puts Nella in a sit and tells her to stay with verbal command and hand gesture (1).
He moves away; Nella is so well trained that she holds the stay even as he turns his back (2).
Brother Christopher tells Nella to come, opening his arms wide in a welcoming gesture (3).
Nella comes running (4) and goes into an automatic sit when she arrives (5).

leash, extending the time to as long as a minute. Then you can start dropping the leash, although it's best to attach a 20-foot length of rope to it so that you can move farther away and still give a correction if you need to.

Be ready to correct your dog as soon as you see the slightest indication that she's about to break the stay. Catch her before she does by stepping toward her and popping the leash straight up to give her the correction, saying "No" and then giving the command to stay again.

The next step is to "proof" the stay by adding distractions. Only do this when you've been working on stay for a number of days and you're completely confident of your dog's ability to hold the position. Walk from side to side, keeping your dog's focus by saying "Watch me" quietly if you need to, pointing to your eye with your first fin-

ger. Jump up and down in front of your dog, and have other people walk by. Toss a hat or a ball nearby. Make a well-timed correction if necessary. Even a well-trained dog may briefly look at the distraction, but if she's really well trained she won't move—and her attention will come right back to you.

Down

Although we've chosen to describe "Down" next, we often teach the "Come" command first, after sit and sit-stay, because most owners give this command from the dog being in a sitting position. But it works just as well from down, and we've placed it here to emphasize the association with stay.

Again, as with stay, this command is sometimes referred to as down-stay. It's a very important command for your dog to master, especially if he's on the larger side. The dog who will hold the down position is under good control and can remain in that position for quite a long period of time—as you chat with a friend on a street corner or even as you prepare a meal in the kitchen.

Some owners have difficulty teaching the down command, and they sometimes become irritated and let an annoyed tone enter their voice. Resist the urge. Down isn't any harder than any of the other commands, and if you follow the techniques explained here, your dog will learn down just as well.

After a short heel, followed by a sit, bend over your dog. Put your right hand behind one of her front legs and your left hand on her shoulders. Start to pull the leg forward and put downward pressure on the shoulders, smoothly easing your dog into the down while saying the command. Stroke her and continue to keep your hand on her back to maintain the position. Praise her but don't be too animated or she will naturally want to bounce back up.

Another way to get your dog into the down position is by using a treat. Take hold of the leash on the side of your dog's neck with your left hand, and show her the treat in your right hand. Bring your right hand down to the ground as you simultaneously add very light downward pressure on the leash. Praise her when she goes into the down position. As she gets better at this, start using the hand gesture only, first with a treat and then without. Praise her warmly.

Once the physical act of going into the down position is mastered, you want to hold her there even when you stand up straight. Do this by stepping lightly on the part of the leash lying on the ground. This will keep your dog from getting up. Keep things brief at first. If she struggles, keep your foot on the leash until she settles. Praise her when she relaxes in the down position, and then release. Review and work more slowly and patiently. Look for her to gradually be able to hold the down for five to ten minutes.

With the down command mastered, you can add a stay command. Proof the down-stay with distractions

such as circling around your dog and stepping back and forth over her. Keep these distractions brief, and praise warmly as she succeeds. The length of the stay can be increased for a longer and longer time so that she can be included at meals, evening television and reading.

Come

The recall command, issued with the word "Come," is something all dog owners want their dogs to be able to do but that many have difficulty teaching. There are three common errors to avoid. First, never try to teach your dog to come if she's loose, not on the leash. You have to be able to enforce the command, and to have

her under control. Second, don't fall into the trap of repeating the command multiple times, which as we already know ends up teaching your dog that she can choose when to obey—or whether to obey at all. Finally, never bring your dog to you in order to chastise her, for having an accident in the house, for example, or for barking too much. Under no circumstances should you associate "Come" with negative consequences. As with all commands, keep things positive.

There are three stages to teaching the recall command. First, put your dog in a sit-stay (or down-stay), and move away to leash length. Bend over slightly and then say the dog's name and the "Come" command in a very animated voice, opening your arms in a welcoming

DOWN-COME

Brother Christopher puts Birgitta in a down and tells her to stay (1). He shows her the hand gesture for stay as he backs away (2). When he tosses his cap to distract her, Birgitta breaks the down-stay (3), indicating she still needs some work. Brother Christopher resets her, and she comes to him when he calls, aided by his hand direction to come right to his feet (4).

gesture. Praise her lavishly if she comes to you, and guide her into a sit as you calm the praise down. If she doesn't come, use the leash to give a quick, short tug, releasing the tension immediately. Keep things upbeat. Don't reel the dog into you; it needs to be her idea that she came to you.

By practicing stage one over the course of several sessions, you've taught your dog the meaning of the command. Now, in stage two, you want to be sure she always comes right to you, without veering off at the last second—as we see quite frequently in dogs who haven't been taught this command properly. Start as you did in stage one, moving out to leash length. Give the command, and as your dog starts coming toward you, you start trotting backwards, keeping the leash slack and

always keeping a few feet between you and the dog. Praise and encourage her as you go. If she starts to veer off to one side as if to pass you, turn slightly in the other direction and give the same slight tug to the leash that you did in stage one, releasing instantly. This will refocus her. Incorporate several of these turning moves, then finally open your arms and welcome the dog close to you, guiding her into a sit. If you practice this backing away through several sessions, you'll avoid the problem of the dog that comes to you—and then keeps going.

Finally, for stage three, you want to teach your dog to come to you over a distance. Attach a 50-foot length of rope or clothesline to the handle end of her leash, with some kind of weight at the other end that will allow you to toss the rope out to its full length. Put your dog in a sit-

stay, then throw the rope. Now back away from your dog, holding your hand out in the stay gesture. When you're about ten feet away, crouch down and call the name and "Come!" As she comes, stand up and funnel your dog into you, and have her sit. As she gets better at this, you can stop crouching down, but still give the welcoming open-arms gesture as you train this command. You can also use a treat held up high to encourage her to go into the sit, but again, don't overdo the treats.

As her performance gets better and better, move farther back along the length of the rope, walking backwards so that you are still facing her. If at any time she doesn't respond or veers away, quickly pick up the rope and use it to correct her, always keeping things upbeat. The correction is never harsh. Eventually you'll be out to the full 50-foot length. Then you can start proofing by introducing distractions, such as other people in the vicinity, or an interesting object like a toy. Also work on not giving the recall command right away; move to the left and right, pacing back and forth, being sure all the time that your dog's attention is focused on you. Then

give the command and, as always, praise her when she gets to you and goes into the sit.

A Final Word

Remember to make formal training a consistent, regular—and, we highly recommend, daily—part of your relationship with your dog. Be patient, and use your judgment as to when you think your dog is ready to move on to a new command. It's always a good idea when teaching something new to start the session with a well-ingrained command, putting your dog in obedience mode before you introduce something less familiar.

Exude confidence. Expect mistakes and don't over-react to them. And show your dog that you are enjoying the process. Those positive vibes will do more than you might imagine to ensure that training is a happy experience for both of you.

Epilogue

"For many of us, love for creation deepens through the relationships we form with our pets, particularly our dogs. By their very nature and need, dogs draw us out of ourselves: they root us in nature, making us more conscious of the mystery of God inherent in all things."

—I & Dog

The paths of dogs and human beings have been intertwined for thousands of years if not longer. Conservative estimates trace the connection to approximately 15,000 years ago, and some researchers even suggest it may go back as much as 135,000 years. From the steppes of Asia and spreading to North America, Europe and beyond, the developing bond has played out in astonishing ways, nurturing and cementing a kinship unlike any other between two species. Both discovered how being in relationship could serve each other's interests, not only in evolutionary terms, but on deeper, more mysterious levels as well. From a human perspective, dogs make us aware that our connections with the natural world go very deep indeed, and that we ignore them at the price of a part of our humanity.

Divine Canine. . .Throughout this book we have told tales of dogs and how they change, how they go from lovable but obstreperous creatures to well-behaved companions, capable of entering into a new type of relationship with their owners. Interestingly, far from quenching a dog's spirit, good training allows it to blossom and thrive. The dog is able to grow toward its potential.

But the training process also affects *us*. Behind each of these stories has always been the human owner, the caregiver entrusted with responsibility for the dog. Whenever we truly follow through on our part of the training, working with attention, consistency and care, a deeper dimension of ourselves gets unlocked, one that sees more than simply a dog obeying, happily following our lead. The relationship has the possibility of moving to the next level, one more difficult to describe. What is worth noticing is how we ourselves change in the midst of this dynamic. We become part of a process of transformation that helps us to become more of who and what we're supposed to be. While some people might scratch their heads at this, what happens in training is very much a part of our true selves emerging, a process of becoming that the dog draws out of us. We become "trained" as well, learning lessons about ourselves that are especially compelling because of the simple guilelessness and honesty of our dogs. Are we alert to what they're saying to us?

Divine Canine . . . Another way of putting this is that a relationship with a dog can be a place of revelation, where God is made manifest in and through the relationship itself, if we would be but open to it. God speaks to us through our dogs—indeed through all life—and woe to us if we're deaf to that voice. The change it stimulates in us has the possibility of being dynamic and continuously interesting; it resists any impulse we might have to think we've ever "arrived," but instead encourages us to go deeper into the relationship.

One of the most important things we've experienced these many years working with dogs is how this work has changed us: They've opened us to the possibility of becoming more patient, more flexible people. They've challenged us to become more responsible, more creative and—forgive our boldness—more loving. Without embarrassment, we suspect we've become better monks and human beings as a result of their presence in our lives. They repeatedly invite us out of ourselves and keep us intimate to the present moment.

Is it not the same for you? Our readers' response to our work over the years leads us to believe it is. Which brings us to a final thought: While we have always tried to avoid romanticizing the relationship between dogs and humans, the reality of what so many of us experience can only have a profound effect on our collective moral and spiritual lives. If such be the case, how can we not be profoundly grateful to our canine friends?

SUGGESTED READING

Our own books:

The Art of Raising a Puppy, by the Monks of New Skete. Little, Brown and Company, 1991.

How to Be Your Dog's Best Friend, by the Monks of New Skete. Little, Brown and Company, revised edition 2002.

I & Dog, by the Monks of New Skete. Yorkville Press, 2003.

Other good sources of information on dogs and dog training:

Adam's Task: Calling Animals by Name
> by Vicki Hearne. Skyhorse Publishing, 2007.

Canine Body Language: A Photographic Guide Interpreting the Native Language of the Domestic Dog
> by Brenda Aloff. Dogwise Publishing, 2005.

The Canine Good Citizen: Every Dog Can Be One
> by Joachim and Wendy Volhard. Howell Book House, 1997.

The Complete Idiot's Guide to a Well-Trained Dog
> by Joachim and Wendy Volhard. Macmillan Distribution, 1999.

Dogs: A Startling New Understanding of Canine Origin, Evolution & Behavior
> by Raymond and Lorna Coppinger. Scribner, 2001.

The Dog's Mind: Understanding Your Dog's Behavior
> by Bruce Fogle. Howell Book House, 1992.

Metrodog: The Essential Guide to Raising Your Dog in the City
> by Brian Kilcommons and Sarah Wilson. Warner Books, 2002.

The Original Dog Bible: The Definitive Source to All Things Dog
> edited by Kristin Mehus-Roe. BowTie Press, 2005.

Paws to Consider: Choosing the Right Dog for You and Your Family
> by Brian Kilcommons and Sarah Wilson. Warner Books, 1999.